The Chameleon in the Room

Embrace Business Risk
Assure Survival & Growth

Chameleons come in many colours and change colour to blend with their background as they hunt insects. Risk also comes in many shades and is often overlooked until it strikes down the unwary and offers the vigilant opportunities.

This book provides practical strategies and tactics for the management of the risks that injure real businesses.

It is unusual in that it provides tools specifically designed to manage those risks that are often ignored by executives; the same risks that have surprised and fatally wounded many giant enterprises, and countless SMEs.

In the face of rapid change and globalisation, data driven risk management methods alone are no longer adequate.

Therefore this text presents alternative ways to cope with the diabolical array of risks that threaten non-financial businesses; including some seldom written about to date e.g. Black Swan Event, Liquidity, External Operational, Concentration, Correlation and Lack of Flexibility Risks.

When adopted, these detailed and illustrated resources will effectively buttress a business against disaster, whatever the entity's size and maturity.

AUTHOR: RON WELLS

PUBLISHED BY: T3P LIMITED

Cover Design and Illustration by Warren Clark
http://warrenclarkgraphicdesign.com

Printed by CreateSpace, an Amazon.com Company

Available from Amazon.com and other retail outlets

Published by: T3P LIMITED

Registered in England & Wales   Co. Number: 4344371
First Floor MIDAS House   Tel: +44 20 8123 0139
62 Goldsworth Road   Email: info@t3plimited.com
Woking Surrey GU21 6LQ   URL: www.t3plimited.com
United Kingdom

First Published July 2015 as a Print Book
Published as an eBook in August 2015

Author: Ron Wells

ISBN: 978-0-9576279-4-9

RON WELLS

Preface

'Every business and every product has risks. You can't get around it.' *Lee Iacocca*

'Only those who risk win. History favours risk-takers - forgets the timid. Everything else is commentary.' *Iveta Cherneva*

The pace and frequency of change has become more of a challenge to the survival of businesses and business models than at any time during the 19th and 20th centuries.

Therefore it is vital to be prepared to deal with 'unexpected and highly consequential' events; often called Black Swan events. Hence the approach to organising Risk Assessment and Management in businesses must be reinvented.

Creating the means for a business to survive the onslaught of known and unknown risks, and thrive - thereby securing jobs in the communities where it operates - is a social and economic imperative.

In this book ideas are offered to assist in the design of Risk Assessment and Management processes to not only protect but also to propel the lasting success of a business enterprise. It is written for executives who work in real businesses that produce, trade, consume or distribute physical commodities, machinery, parts and equipment or consumer products and services.

It is not aimed at pure financial businesses of which Henry Ford said;

'A Business that makes nothing but money is a poor kind of business.'

Ron Wells
CGMA ACMA FCIS ACIB CCE
Passionate Promoter of Holistic
Future Oriented Risk Management

Embrace Business Risk Assure Survival & Growth

RISK MANAGEMENT IN REAL BUSINESSES

Chapter 1

Unknown Unknowns – Potentially the Most Damaging
Risk outcomes that are triggered by highly significant events that cannot be anticipated because they have not occurred in the past

Unknown Knowns – Outcomes that Injure Businesses
Risk outcomes that often occur in the ordinary course of business; probabilities are known but specifics as to which outcomes will arise are not known.

Known Unknowns – Appraised using Stress Testing
Risk outcomes that can be imagined and the probability exaggerated to aid contingency planning.

RISKS THAT OFTEN KILL REAL BUSINESSES

Chapter 2

Black Swan Events

Unknown Unknowns / Unquantifiable Uncertainty

Calculating Corporate Probable Maximum Loss (CPML)
Preparing to manage a Black Swan Event, illustrated with an
example based on the Volkswagen Group

Past Black Swan Events with Global Impact

Chapter 3

Liquidity Risk

The Risk that destroyed Lehman Brothers and sparked the
2008 Credit Crisis

Hedging Future Commodity Price Risk can Damage the
Liquidity of a Real Business
Potential Loss of Competitive Position
Hedging and Margining

Assessing and Managing Liquidity Risk
Liquidity Risk in Financial Institutions
Liquidity Risk in Physical Businesses
Frozen Working Capital Management and the Success
Paradox

Cash Flow Cycle Greed Control Example
Corus Group Plc 2002 to 2005

Medium and Long Term Liquidity Risk Management in Real
Businesses

Infrastructure Projects – Staged Payment Commitments

Chapter 4

Operational Risk

The Risk that almost destroyed Ericsson in March 2000
Toyota profit slides on Japan earthquake disruption
Worst Thai Floods in 50 Years hit Toyota Supply Chain

Managing Operational Risk

External Event Driven Operational Risk Management

Limiting Supply-Chain Related Damage
The Process Illustrated with an Example

Chapter 5

Concentration Risk and Correlation Risk

Geographic Concentration & Correlation Risk Example

Chapter 6

Lack of Flexibility and Agility

The Enemies of Agility – Ignored External Change

The Agents of Agility
Empowerment and Organisation Structure
Imagination and Innovation
Freelancing and Sharing Business Resources (SBR)

Change and Business in the Future

RISK TOOLS FOR UNKNOWN UNKNOWNS

The risk assessment and management tools available to executives who will be responsible for the ongoing viability of a physical business when an unimaginable event strikes

Chapter 7

Courage – Decisions without Data

Imagining the Future

Fictional Illustration:
A Business Decision Thought Process

Chapter 8

Scenario Planning

The Scenario Planning Process

An Example Scenario: How will our 9.2 billion neighbours be gainfully employed in 2035?

RISKS THAT INJURE REAL BUSINESSES

Other than macro- and micro- unimaginable events there are several categories of risk that may attack and injure real businesses, by causing losses. Generally executives are prepared to effectively deal with these risks using tried and tested techniques. This section covers the most common forms of these risks.

Chapter 9

BIBLIOGRAPHY

RISK MANAGEMENT IN REAL BUSINESSES

The nature of the many varied risks that can affect real businesses and the suggested approach to apply in order to effectively manage the risks is covered in this section. Real businesses produce, trade, consume or distribute physical commodities, machinery, parts and equipment or consumer products and services.

It has become fashionable to import many of the risk assessment and management practices operated by financial institutions into the real business sphere. Those practices that have proven to be ineffective in this context are described, together with appropriate alternative methods.

Chapter 1

Managing the Future – Making Decisions

Decisions and Risk

Decisions, Risk and the Future are a package; they cannot be considered separately or isolated from one another. Decisions incorporate Risk and lead to outcomes that occur or do not occur in the Future.

Risk is defined in most English dictionaries in terms of loss, danger, peril, hazard, threat or menace; all concepts with negative connotations.

However Risk essentially describes the occurrence of an unexpected, unanticipated or surprise outcome to a planned or forecast series of events. Therefore Risk is more akin to Adventure than to Danger.

Indeed one translation of Risk rendered in Chinese, provided by Google Translate, is Mào-Xiǎn (冒险) a word consisting of two symbols (or syllables) each of which separately is also translated to mean Risk. Hence Mào-Xiǎn can be translated as Risk-Risk; bringing to mind the Chinese preference for two syllable words, which is usually achieved by repeating the same character rather than different characters with the same prima facie meaning.

According to the Berlitz Pocket Dictionary, on the other hand, Adventure is correctly translated as Mào-Xiǎn. Thus underlining the proposition that Risk - like an Adventure - should be thought of as harbouring both positive and negative elements, both opportunities and threats; Risk-Plus and Risk-Minus concepts, hence two different characters each with a subtly different meaning.

The Point

Decisions are made in light of (a) all known information and (b) a judgement as to the likely influence of unknown information on the desired outcome. Therefore decisions are the result of a 'best guess' as to what should be done or avoided in order to achieve a desired result. Given the unknown elements at the time a decision is taken and the consequent action is initiated, there is a risk that the desired outcome will not be achieved.

Making a Decision is 'Taking a Risk' in an effort
to 'Manage the Future'.

Managing the Future

The Future does not exist.
The Past existed.
Only the Present exists.

We can remember the Past, and often re-write it to suit our own ends but we cannot know the Future, because it does not exist.

The Future will never exist, only the Present exists.

Of course Time is an intellectual concept that admittedly is perceived differently in various cultures within the human family. Richard Lewis of Richard Lewis Communications in his June 1, 2014 Business Insider article titled *'How Different Cultures Understand Time'* described three such variations thus:

"In the **linear-active**, industrialised Western cultures time is seen as a road along which we proceed. Life is sometimes referred to as a 'journey'; death is often referred to as the 'end of the road.' We imagine ourselves as having travelled along the part of the road that is behind us (the past) and we see the untrodden path of the future stretching out in front of us.

Linear-oriented people do not regard the future as entirely unknowable for they have already nudged it along certain channels by meticulous planning.

Cyclic time is not seen as a straight road leading from our feet to the horizon, but as a curved one which in one year's time will lead us through 'scenery' and conditions very similar to what we experience at the present moment. Observers of cyclic time are less disciplined in their planning of the future, since they believe that it cannot be managed and that humans make life easier for themselves by 'harmonising' with the laws and cyclic events of nature. Yet in such cultures a general form of planning is still possible, for many things are fairly regular and well understood.

In Madagascar, the opposite is the case. The Malagasy imagine the future as flowing into the back of their heads, or passing them from behind, then becoming the past as it stretches out in front of them. The past is in front of their eyes because it is visible, known and influential. They can look at it, enjoy it, learn from it, (and) even 'play with it.'

(Thus) by contrast, the Malagasy consider the future unknowable. It is behind their head where they do not have eyes. Their plans for this unknown area will be far from meticulous, for what can they be based on?"

Since we live in the Present we can assume that the Future will never exist for us, hence only the Present exists; when the Future arrives it will be the Present.

Nonetheless the Future comes from and begins in the Present, and carries with it the 'baggage' of the Past. That baggage both constrains the Future and provides pointers as to the shape and content of the Future.

In the prophetic words of William Gibson in 1993:

"The future is already here — it's just not evenly distributed."

Contrary to what Mr Gibson said later, developments that are occurring beyond the mainstream today can easily be uncovered by searching the web, so are definitely 'Google-able'.

Nevertheless Managing the Future requires Courage and Imagination.

Courage, because every decision maker must overcome the fear of being wrong.

In the words of Mark Twain:

"Courage is resistance to fear, mastery of fear,
not absence of fear"

Imagination, because the Future as it may affect the outcome of a decision at hand must be imagined, based on a combination of the researched facts uncovered and intuition.

"It takes Courage to take a Risk not Numbers"
Life's a Pitch: Stephen Bayley & Roger Mavity

Numbers

In the business world Numbers and their associates Statistics are collected and manipulated by those revered historians the Accountants and Quantitative Analysts (Quant's).

Accountants spend their time collecting numbers, and manipulating them to fit into standardised rules so that every company can be compared with every other company regardless of how different each company's business model may be from those of all other companies. They also presume to 'model the Future' by producing in infinite detail budgets and targets against which the business will be managed and measured for the next fiscal period. Such budgets are often a

14

straight-jacket for the business since they are always based on the broad and inevitably erroneous assumption that 'the next period will be a repeat of the last period only somewhat better'.

Needless to say the historic accounting record of what has happened in a business is produced based on an accounting schedule so, for the most part, is of no use to decision makers who must manage day to day.

In the context of Managing the Future such numbers only provide some indication of the foundation upon which a business stands, its business model (how it makes money) and the competency or otherwise of its management.

Prudent analysts will bear in mind that all Financial Statements and Reports are manipulated by the management in order to 'tell the story' they want the users of those statements to learn, not to tell the whole story; whether Audited or not, and whether based on GAAP or IAS standards or not.

International Accounting Standards allow 'management discretion' to decide the treatment and presentation of key numbers. As a result financial reports are peppered with statements such as this: "These assumptions are based on the best estimates and judgments made by management…"

Auditors usually add a statement to their report that reads: "An audit also includes evaluating the appropriateness of accounting policies used and the reasonableness of accounting estimates made by management…" That simply means that the Auditors are satisfied that the IAS rules have been followed, it does not mean that the management have chosen the least favourable option available under the rules.

In any event financial accounts are historical documents that cannot be an adequate basis for decision making relating to the future. For example, it would be folly to base a decision to deliver goods to a customer on open account terms (unsecured) solely on the basis of a set of ratios calculated from its financial statements. Incompetent or dishonest management will cause the strongest company to fail in the future, which is when payment will be received or not.

Quant's specialise in building mathematical models, which rely mainly on probability theories and are based on statistical data.

Unfortunately a naïve belief that mathematical models can foretell future risks in the spheres of economics, finance and commerce has become current. This belief has arisen largely through the use by Investment Banks of models on the basis of which they have traded financial instruments.

As G E Pelham Box (1919–2013) a Professor of Statistics said:

"Essentially, all models are wrong, but some are useful."

Models cannot foretell the future in these fields, simply because there are too many variables at play and the models are derived from data that occurred in the past.

"Many people in various fields tend to follow the Young method. If they are studying economics, or the human body and health, or the workings of the brain, they tend to work with abstractions and simplifications, reducing highly complex and interactive problems into modules, formulas, tidy statistics, and isolated organs that can be dissected. This approach can yield a partial picture of reality, much in the way that dissecting a corpse can tell you some things about the human body. But with these simplifications the living, breathing element is missing.

You want to follow instead the Champollion model. You are not in a hurry. You prefer the holistic approach. You look at the object of study from as many angles as possible, giving your thoughts added dimensions. You assume that the parts of any whole interact with one another and cannot be completely separated. In your mind, you get as close to the complicated truth and reality of your object of study as possible. In the process, great mysteries will unravel themselves before your eyes."

This passage from the book *Mastery* written by Robert Greene, refers to the limitations of the formulaic, mathematics-based approach to studying what are now called 'Complex Systems'.

Complex Systems are systems that operate on the basis of so many random variables that they cannot be successfully expressed within mathematical models. In creating models Quant's make certain fixed assumptions – e.g. that all shoppers make rational purchase decisions – and strictly limit the number of variables incorporated. Subsequently most users of the output of such models do not know on what assumptions they are based so cannot judge to what extent those assumptions have skewed the output. Other limitations include the reliance on data – using what happened in the past to predict the future – and ignoring other potentially influential variables, and discounting outlying data – data points that occurred in the past more than three standard deviations beyond the mean. The latter are considered likely to occur only once every 125 years, they are the so-called Black Swans or Fat Tail occurrences that in reality have happened much more frequently and are the sort of risks that have caused multiple business failures.

The global economy is a Complex System since it is created and influenced by the actions and decisions of billions of global citizens. Each action and decision is potentially a random variable.

Chaos theory asserts that a relatively small change in a series, near its starting point, leads to a significantly different outcome.

Risk, particularly business related risk, is a Complex System because it is impacted by many variables both within a business entity and external to a business.

Therefore Risk at the enterprise level should not be managed on the basis of potential outcomes derived from mathematical models. It should rather be based on a holistic assessment of the forces shaping the future viability of the enterprise. Furthermore risk management processes and survival action plans should be built on the same holistic foundation.

OW Bunker A/S, the Danish shipping-fuel supplier went from a US$1bn valuation after its initial public offering in March 2014 to bankruptcy in November 2014 mainly due to an alleged fraud perpetrated in its Singapore office. This is an example of the occurrence of a fatal risk that could not have been predicted using financial modelling.

As G E Pelham Box (1919–2013) a Professor of Statistics said:

"Essentially, all models are wrong, but some are useful."

Useful Numerical Models and ScoreCards

Executives of real businesses do find some mathematical models and ScoreCards useful. In general such models will be those that provide a signal that an investigation or analysis should be initiated in order to determine if action should be taken to avoid or reduce a risk, or to seize an opportunity.

Examples discussed in more detail in this book include:

- Concentration Risk Analysis
- Correlation Risk Analysis
- Liquidity Risk analysis and management based on cash flow forecasting and risk assessment
- Portfolio Analysis and Management, based on Risk Scoring
- Limiting and Pricing Risk based on Probability of Default estimations (i.e. ensuring adequate margins when unsecured credit is granted)

RISKS THAT OFTEN KILL REAL BUSINESSES

The risks classed as Unknown Unknowns or Unquantifiable Uncertainties are described in this section. This is the risk category that has most often fatally wounded real businesses.

Generally executives are not prepared to effectively deal with these particular risks when they strike.

Chapter 2

Black Swan Events

Unquantifiable Uncertainty / Unknown Unknowns

The most dangerous risk that lies hidden within every business is extreme tail risk. In his seminal book *Managing Extreme Financial Risk - Strategies and Tactics (to ensure the survival of) Going Concerns*, first published in 2013, Karamjeet Paul wrote about the risk associated with Unknown Unknowns, and coined the highly descriptive phrase 'Unquantifiable Uncertainty'. Later he wrote an article for Forbes Opinion in which he inter alia explained the genesis of this risk; part of his article is quoted here, paraphrased to adapt it to apply to corporate entities rather than financial institutions:

"There are infinite combinations of factors that could strain a (company's) capital. Humans are only capable of imagining a small fraction of these. Therefore, no simulation can envision all possible scenarios, and thus prepare for 'unexpected and highly consequential' events, also known as Black Swan events, that stress testing does not address.

Even though Black Swans can't be predicted, Nassim Nicholas Taleb, an authority on Black Swans and professor of risk engineering at NYU says that 'through some mental bias, people think in hindsight that they *sort of* considered the possibility of such events; this gives them confidence in continuing to formulate predictions. But our tools for forecasting and risk measurement cannot begin to capture Black Swans. Indeed, our faith in these tools makes it more likely that we will continue to take dangerous, uninformed risks.'

The combination of this mental bias and passing stress tests can lull organisations into believing they can survive extreme crises or Black Swans. A similar complacent mindset existed before 2008 as managers and regulators monitored banks via

VaR, a then-fashionable statistical measure of maximum possible losses, without appreciating its severe limitations. This proved not only useless in dealing with **the crash**, but also may have created a false sense of security pre-2008.

Relying only on stress testing, even though it is a critical component of uncertainty management, nevertheless leaves most institutions unprepared for extreme adversity. Uncertainty is defined by possible outcomes and the probabilities of such possible outcomes. Therefore the spectrum of uncertainty can be divided into four parts, each needing a different solution.

First, known outcomes with known certainty, or 'Known-Knowns,' are easy to deal with (since there is no uncertainty).

Second, situations where specific outcomes are unknown, but their probabilities are known, or 'Unknown-Knowns,' can be handled by using known probabilities to calculate expected losses, which can be covered by pricing premiums. This is traditional risk management (as practiced by many sophisticated corporate entities, aping financial institutions).

Third, situations where outcomes can be defined and are thus known, but their probabilities are unknown, or 'Known-Unknowns,' can be addressed by preparing to deal with the impact of known scenarios. This is 'stress testing'.

Fourth, situations where both outcomes and probabilities are unknown - 'Unknown-Unknowns - (are the most challenging) as they can't be envisioned; Black Swans arise from Unknown-Unknowns."

Extracted from *What Stress Testing is Not* a Forbes Opinion Article by Karamjeet Paul published 2014.09.22

Although Black Swan events that are of global import receive a lot of attention and are widely examined after they occur, real businesses can also be subject to explicit, localised or industry specific Black Swan events. A disruptive technology or invention that appropriates a particular market is one example of the type of Unknown-Unknown that would only affect a sub-set of businesses. Uber taxi services have the potential to destroy the monopoly held since 1865 by licenced London Black Cab drivers; each of whom has qualified in *the knowledge* of the city's geography by means of up to two years of pre-qualification study.

To date the risk that losses could be experienced as a result of Unknown-Unknowns occurring has largely been ignored in both the Financial Institution and Corporate sectors.

It has been unconsciously assumed that;

- Such incidents occur so rarely that they can safely be ignored and/or

- Such incidents cannot be imagined since they have never happen before they happen, therefore it is not possible to anticipate the loss that may result and/or

- It is not possible to plan an effective coping strategy to ensure survival and continued operations since the nature of such an incident cannot be known.

Generally speaking corporate executives are therefore unprepared should an Unquantifiable Uncertainty strike; in such cases the corporate entities' equity capital becomes the last line of defence against bankruptcy.

Karamjeet Paul, writing about financial institutions, pointed out that this is not a satisfactory situation in that context and it certainly is not satisfactory in the corporate context.

Having recognised this Unquantifiable Uncertainty risk category it is sensible to endeavour to anticipate the potential maximum future loss that could result from such an occurrence, and to think through and discuss possible defensive measures that could be taken in order to protect an entity's capital and ongoing concern status.

The aim of such preparation would be to arm executives with an array of possible action steps that could be tailored to any situation that may arise, thus enabling them (a) to react immediately and effectively in any extreme situation and thereby (b) to be in a position to capitalise on the opportunities that are bound to arise in the wake of such situations.

Calculating Corporate Probable Maximum Loss

In the case of the occurrence of a Black Swan event it is not possible to quantify the expected loss mathematically since no relevant data exists. However in relation to a business entity the maximum loss that can be sustained before its existence is extinguished is in effect the total book value of its Assets. That is equivalent to total Liabilities plus Capital and Reserves.

The administrator of a business liquidated in the aftermath of a Black Swan event would repay secured and unsecured liabilities to the extent possible; then any residue funds would be distributed to the equity owners.

Therefore it is submitted that despite the fact that Black Swan events cannot be imagined and hence the consequences cannot be evaluated, senior executives should discuss and agree survival plans for immediate implementation when one occurs.

As a first planning step the size of the challenge can be estimated by aggregating the 'forced sale' net disposable value of the entity's assets; which could be referred to as the 'Maximum Covered Liabilities' (MCL) if no management action is initiated. In other words the MCL is the amount of the liabilities that can be paid using asset sale proceeds, the balance of the liabilities plus equity and reserves can be termed the 'Maximum Uncovered Liabilities' (MUL).

The MUL minus the Equity Capital could be referred to as the 'Owner Protection Gap' (OPG).

Preparation for dealing with a Black Swan event should focus on identifying actions that could be taken to reduce the OPG in the face of an Extreme Risk situation.

Preparing to manage a Black Swan Event, illustrated with an example based on the Volkswagen Group

Consider this fictitious example created by the author, based on the Consolidated Financial Statements of the Volkswagen Group as of December 31, 2013:

€ 324.3 bn	Total Assets at book value on the 'going concern' basis
€ 141.5 bn	Net Realisable Value (**NRV**) of total assets under 'forced sale' conditions
€ 182.8 bn	Maximum Uncovered Liabilities including Equity (**MUL**)
€ 90.0 bn	Equity
€ 92.8 bn	Owner Protection Gap (**OPG**)

The MUL figure is useful because it provides an expression of the maximum possible size of the challenge VW would face should an Extreme Risk event occur. It is a number that can be tracked, reported to the Board Risk Committee and considered by the Senior Executive when finalising Business Continuity Plans. Calculating and reporting the MUL regularly effectively 'puts Fat Tail or Extreme Risk on the agenda' and ensures that this previously ignored risk and its potential to kill the business receives serious attention.

In summary it is a means to encourage those executives required to take action when a Black Swan event strikes, to regularly engage in discussions as to what defensive steps would be taken and by whom.

The joint creation of a palette of action steps to be taken by those with this responsibility will enable immediate execution and avoid lengthy argumentative 'crisis meetings', which would be likely to cause opportunities to be missed.

Executives should simultaneously give thought to the opportunities that might become evident in a Black Swan scenario. They should be prepared to take advantage of such instances.

The purchase of Bear Stearns (including its valuable New York office building) in the midst of an Extreme Risk crisis in 2008 is an example of a survivor (J P Morgan Chase) taking over a failing competitor based on 'fire sale' asset values; asset values were falling rapidly as inter-bank credit evaporated and banks frantically chased cash to meet margin calls and other obligations falling due.

In the context of this VW example, group executives - having noted that all Intangible Assets are assigned zero value in the NRV calculation - may conclude that the sale of certain Brands at near full value could be possible if action were taken early enough in the course of a crisis.

Based on five times Operating Profits generated by the Audi, ŠKODA, Bentley, Porsche and Scania brands in 2013, VW Group could raise as much as € 23 billion from their sale; thus potentially reducing the Owner Protection Gap (OPG) by 25%.

Note that the author has no inside knowledge of VW Group so this example is simply an educated guess as to a contingent action that may be proposed; no doubt VW executives would have many ideas.

Past Black Swan Events with Global Impact

1990 US High Yield (HY) bond market collapses

1991 Oil price surge

1992 Swedish banking crisis

1994 Mexican crisis

1997 Asian crisis

1998 Russia default, Rouble crash, Long-Term Capital Management LP (LTCM) collapse

2000 TMT (Technology Media & Telecoms) collapse (a.k.a. Dot-com Bubble)

2001 9/11 payment system disruption

2002 Argentina crisis

2004 Russian banking crisis, Indian Ocean tsunami

2008 Global credit crisis

2010 Greece

2011 Japan triple tragedy – force 9 quake, massive tsunami and Fukushima nuclear melt-down / Thailand floods

2014 Rouble and Oil Price in free-fall

2015 Euro – Swiss Franc (EUR-CHF) exchange rate CAP removed

Each of these events was unique and caused financial institutions and real businesses to incur significant losses. Many subsequently failed, most often as a direct result of lack of Liquidity (no access to cash) and/or disrupted supply chains (Operational issues) resulting in lack of inventory negatively impacting revenue.

Chapter 3

Liquidity Risk

The Risk that destroyed Lehman Brothers and sparked the 2008 Credit Crisis

Lehman Brothers suffered a severe liquidity crisis in September 2008, a crisis that led directly to its demise. Initially the market, aware that Lehman had reported massive losses and was operating with borrowed funds amounting to thirty-one times its equity, lost confidence in Lehman Brothers' ability to survive as a going concern and withheld credit, thus starving it of liquidity. At the same time its counterparties – mainly other financial institutions with which it had outstanding derivatives contracts, fearing Lehman would fail to honour such contracts were progressively calling on Lehman to provide them with more cash collateral, generally known as 'variation margin' or simply 'margin'.

Desperate to meet margin calls (demands) Lehman Brothers commenced a 'fire sale' of its assets to raise cash. This set off a vicious cycle, as assets were offered to the market the purchase bid prices sank ever lower – as those assets remaining in Lehman's portfolio were revalued for accounting purposes at the lower prices – its credit rating was revised downwards and immediately new margin calls demanding more cash were triggered. Unable to stem the deluge of margin calls and unable to persuade the authorities to provide the billions of US Dollars required to ensure survival, Lehman Brothers was forced into bankruptcy protection on September 15th.

Speaking in New York on May 28, 2015 Lehman's former chief executive, Richard Fuld Jr confirmed that a lack of liquidity was the true culprit behind Lehman's demise: "You have to have enough liquidity to ride out the storm. Been there - Done that - No comment." (Channel NewsAsia)

The fallout that ensued in the wake of Lehman's collapse negatively affected the lives and livelihoods of millions of people in every corner of the Globe, and will continue to do so for at least a decade.

It is tempting to think that the scenario that brought down Lehman Brothers could only happen to a financial institution trading in derivatives and other complex financial products but that is not the case. Many real businesses hedge future price risk for sound reasons and find they are liable to provide daily adjusted amounts of cash or Standby Letter of Credit (SBLC) collateral to the hedge protection provider.

Hedging future commodity price risk is something to consider, only if the concomitant Liquidity Risk is carefully managed and the competitive position of the business is unlikely to be negatively affected.

Some Hedging Jargon

The term 'Hedging' has been adopted into financial parlance because it succinctly describes the act of sheltering from danger or risk; as if by hiding in or behind a hedge.

Businesses 'Hedge' to protect themselves against potential losses that could be directly or indirectly caused by commodity price changes in the future.

There are two types of hedging generally available to commercial businesses;

- Direct Physical Hedge (DPH) and
- Indirect Financial Hedge (IFH).

Hedging a 'Short Position' refers to fixing the cost of purchasing a certain volume or amount of a commodity or index price related product at a point in time in the future. An airline operator that is selling already priced tickets for travel six months in the future could, for example, fix the cost of the aviation fuel it will require to operate the flights in question by contracting a DPH with a fuel supplier or trader, or an IFH with a financial institution.

Hedging a 'Long Position' refers to fixing the price at which to sell a certain volume or amount of a commodity or index price related product at a point in time in the future. A smelter in Germany that produces aluminium by means of a continuous process and has a fairly stable cost base, could fix the price at which it will sell its output in the future by hedging through the London Metal Exchange (LME) for example. The LME operates a physically settled exchange but obligations to deliver metal can be settled financially if preferred.

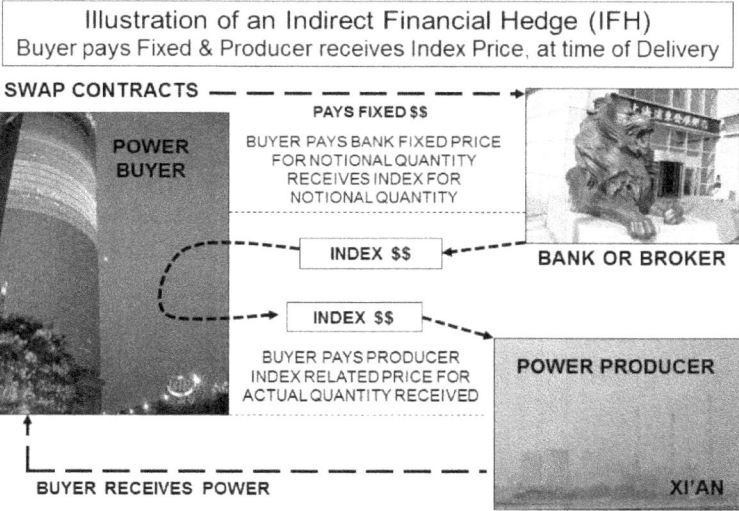

Illustration of an Indirect Financial Hedge (IFH)
Buyer pays Fixed & Producer receives Index Price, at time of Delivery

SWAP CONTRACTS

POWER BUYER

PAYS FIXED $$
BUYER PAYS BANK FIXED PRICE FOR NOTIONAL QUANTITY RECEIVES INDEX FOR NOTIONAL QUANTITY

INDEX $$

BANK OR BROKER

INDEX $$

BUYER PAYS PRODUCER INDEX RELATED PRICE FOR ACTUAL QUANTITY RECEIVED

POWER PRODUCER

BUYER RECEIVES POWER

XI'AN

The prices of many commodities (mainly energy and raw material inputs) are determined by the global supply and demand balance, as it is perceived by traders and investors. Commodity prices fluctuate as traders and investors buy or sell related financial instruments on international exchanges. The cost basis of all goods and services is impacted directly or indirectly by the ebb and flow of the demand/supply balance reflected by related commodity price fluctuations. Therefore the costs of producing 'downstream' goods and services change frequently and unpredictably as international commodity prices continuously rise and fall.

Oil prices affect transport costs; oil, coal and gas prices affect power and heating costs; steel, iron ore and coking coal prices affect construction costs; aluminium, steel and resin costs affect machinery and vehicle manufacturing costs; corn and soybean prices affect animal feed costs, which with urea (fertiliser) costs affect food prices.

In this way all consumed goods and services are connected to basic commodities, most of which are priced with reference to international exchange traded financial instruments.

Hedging Future Commodity Price Risk can Damage the Liquidity of a Real Business

Whether a producer of an energy or base metal commodity, or a consumer of wholesale quantities of natural gas, electricity, coal, aviation fuel, diesel, aluminium, copper, platinum or palladium, sugar, coffee, cocoa, corn, soybeans, frozen orange juice, pork bellies, palm oil or urea (for example) the prospect of fixing the future price at which to sell or source such commodity is very attractive. This is especially the case for a Financial Accountant, who is keen to produce an 'accurate' three year budget.

However dangers lurk in such a strategy;

- First there is the risk that the hedge will give competitors an advantage,
- Second there is the risk of counterparty future failure (failure of the supplier, customer or financial hedge provider to perform its contract obligations), and
- Third the risk that margining, if any, will impact liquidity in unexpected ways.

Potential Loss of Competitive Position

If a physical business hedges and its competitor does not, it will either win or lose; that is, if market prices move against it, its competitor will capitalise on the price advantage it enjoys and the hedged business will stand to lose market share and profit.

On the other hand, if prices move in favour of the hedged business (that is to say the hedge protects it from an adverse price movement) it will be able to trump any unhedged competitor, at least in the short term.

A real business usually has two ways to protect itself from future price movements that would have a negative impact on its net revenue, namely:

- Selling the goods it produces, purchases and/or wholesales at a fixed price agreed on the date of contract, with delivery scheduled to occur on a future date, and/or

- Buying the goods it purchases and/or wholesales at a fixed price agreed on the date of the contract, with receipt of the goods scheduled to occur on a future date,

  OR

- Agreeing a derivative with a financial institution or other provider, designed to provide a sum on maturity sufficient to compensate the business for any deterioration in income it would otherwise have suffered due to an adverse market reference price movement.

The win or lose 'gamble' vis-à-vis competitors is the reason many businesses either decline to hedge (decline to agree fixed price future delivery or supply contracts, or derivatives that achieve the same end) or hedge only a proportion of requirements.

Airline operators are a well-publicised example of a business type that often hedges, seeking to fix the cost of aviation fuel in an effort to protect profit margins against future upward movements in the industry's most cost volatile input. Hedged operators are then unable to take advantage of dips in the price of fuel and therefore not able to concurrently reduce fares, much to the chagrin of the general public. An example of this occurred during the eight month period from June 2014 when the Brent Crude Oil Futures price dropped from around US$115 per barrel to US$48 per barrel in late January 2015. Those airline operators that had fortuitously hedged less of their requirements for that period than their direct competitors naturally had a cost advantage as a result.

Hedging and Margining

As noted above a business that makes the decision to hedge its price risk when selling a product faces customer risk in two respects; namely, performance risk and payment risk.

If it is a buyer, the hedging business incurs counterparty (contract party) performance risk exposure.

Physical Business Customer Risk Splits into Performance Risk and Payment Risk

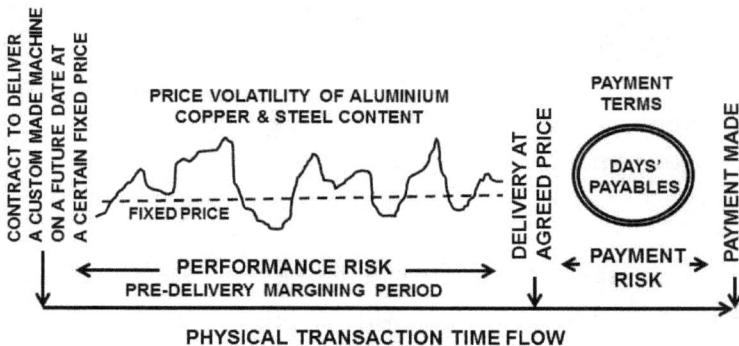

PHYSICAL TRANSACTION TIME FLOW

Performance risk can be assigned a direct monetary value daily - by reference to market prices - in order to deduce the difference between the fixed price contract (hedge) and the current market value of the underlying commodity that is to be delivered, sold or purchased in the future. This is the marked-to-market (m2m) value of the contract each day and the actual amount that would be lost (or gained) if the contract was not honoured and the physical delivery had to be replaced by purchase or sale in the market on that day. Hence the m2m value is the quantum of exposure that one party to a hedge has to the other, its counterparty. This approach assumes the existence of a liquid market in the commodity and at the place of delivery in question.

In the case of a physical business (as opposed to a purely financial business) the requirement that a liquid market in the commodity hedged must exist at the intended place of physical delivery cannot be over-emphasised. The term 'liquid market' in this case means a market for the commodity in question at the place in question that consists of sufficient willing buyers and sufficient willing sellers, contracting sufficient numbers of transactions, to ensure a substitute deal to replace a failed transaction can be struck at a fair market price.

Consider the case of a Brazilian exporter of soybeans to China that arranges an IFH created using a Soybean Futures Contract through the Chicago Board of Trade (CBOT) commodities exchange; in order to fix its target selling price and profit margin. The cargo is then loaded on a ship that arrives in Shanghai 32 days later, only two days after the Chinese buyer is declared bankrupt.

When closed the hedge 'pays' or 'charges' the seller the difference between the seller's target selling price and the current price for the Soybean Futures Contract quoted on the CBOT exchange.

The seller had contracted to sell the soybean cargo at the ruling CBOT exchange quoted price on the day it was delivered in Shanghai. The perishable cargo is unfortunately now effectively stranded in Shanghai so the seller is unlikely to realise the internationally quoted price. Instead the seller will have to urgently find an alternative buyer with the necessary authority to import the cargo so will probably have to accept a large discount to the internationally quoted price.

Hence the seller is likely to realise a loss on the cargo and will probably also have to pay additional freight (demurrage) to the shipper because the ship will spend more time in Shanghai than expected.

This is an example of the way in which losses can arise despite a hedge being in place, when a physical cargo is stranded in an illiquid physical market environment.

If a business has a margining agreement with its counterparty, and its position on any day is 'out of the money' (meaning the business would owe its counterparty money if the deal were terminated immediately) and the amount the business would owe exceeds the agreed threshold (effectively a credit limit) it would have to post variation margin. That is to pay cash or provide an SBLC (if allowed in the agreement) to its counterparty, equal to the difference between the amount that would be owed and the threshold.

How prices may move cannot be predicted – that is the reason a margin agreement is put in place, it provides mutual protection since it is usually a two-way agreement. However this means that business executives cannot predict how much cash or committed SBLC facility may be required from day to day, in order to provide margin. To make matters worse, often margin agreement thresholds are tied to credit ratings or financial strength covenants, so if the credit standing of a business deteriorates the amount of margin that will have to be posted could increase rapidly, which is an unpredictable possibility.

Initial Margin

A hedging arrangement that is made using a financial derivative instrument, an IFH, will usually require the business to pay an Initial Margin (IM). An IM is a cash deposit given to the Bank or Broker providing the hedge, before transactions are initiated. It is subsequently held by the bank as long as trading continues. The Bank or Broker is also known as a 'Clearing Member' if the derivative is traded on an Exchange.

The IM amount can be changed on demand by the Bank or Broker.

The initial margin cash provides the Bank or Broker with a reserve amount to use to cover (recoup) any losses that may be incurred if its client's position is prematurely closed. A contracted position may be prematurely closed, for example, if a client fails to pay a margin call.

At that moment the variation margin (VM) that the Bank will have collected prior to the default will probably be insufficient to cover the final settlement amount. This is so because VM is collected daily, based on the closing reference price the previous day; hence the reference price will have changed since the last VM call amount was received. The reference price will continue to change during the three to ten days that it takes to finally close the positions, so the VM already held by the Bank may ultimately be insufficient to reimburse its loss. In such a case the IM amount will be used to clear the balance due to the Bank or Broker.

A Bank, Broker or Exchange will only rarely accept Standby Letters of Credit (SBLCs) or Bank Guarantees instead of cash, as Initial Margin.

Mathematical models can provide some 'worst case' future scenarios on which basis an estimate can be made of potential liquidity requirements. However the models available assume that the future will resemble the past. Unfortunately negative

Black Swan events – the very events that cause massive price volatilities and could seriously damage liquidity - cannot be predicted by mathematical means.

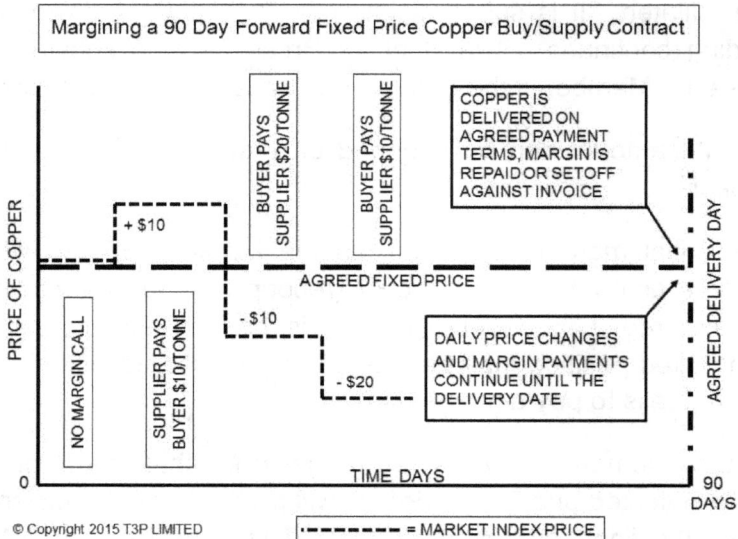

Margining a 90 Day Forward Fixed Price Copper Buy/Supply Contract

BUYER PAYS SUPPLIER $20/TONNE

BUYER PAYS SUPPLIER $10/TONNE

COPPER IS DELIVERED ON AGREED PAYMENT TERMS, MARGIN IS REPAID OR SETOFF AGAINST INVOICE

PRICE OF COPPER

+ $10

AGREED FIXED PRICE

- $10

- $20

NO MARGIN CALL

SUPPLIER PAYS BUYER $10/TONNE

DAILY PRICE CHANGES AND MARGIN PAYMENTS CONTINUE UNTIL THE DELIVERY DATE

AGREED DELIVERY DAY

TIME DAYS

0

90 DAYS

© Copyright 2015 T3P LIMITED

-------- = MARKET INDEX PRICE

Lehman Brothers' inability to pay its margin calls due to lack of immediately available cash ultimately caused its demise. Therefore it is imperative to understand and monitor daily the possible negative implications of any margin agreements that exist, and to actively negotiate such agreements to maximise contracted thresholds and minimise the possible escalation of 'calls' if negative events occur.

Furthermore it is advisable to negotiate additional standby 'committed' credit lines with house banks, to cover short-term needs that may arise; although so-called committed lines are seldom truly irrevocable therefore the terms and conditions should be carefully scrutinised.

Tight control must nevertheless be exercised over any derivatives portfolio held by a business. All hedges contracted must relate closely to physical transactions, and the reference prices used in determining settlement amounts must correlate closely to the price movements associated with the physical transactions covered. In other words, the creation of speculative 'open' (un-hedged) derivative positions must be avoided. Only on this basis can it be accepted that hedged positions will be self-liquidating when they mature.

Contracting un-hedged derivative agreements is tantamount to gambling.

Regardless of the controls in place the day to day liquidity implications of hedging have to be managed during open exposure periods, if margining is required.

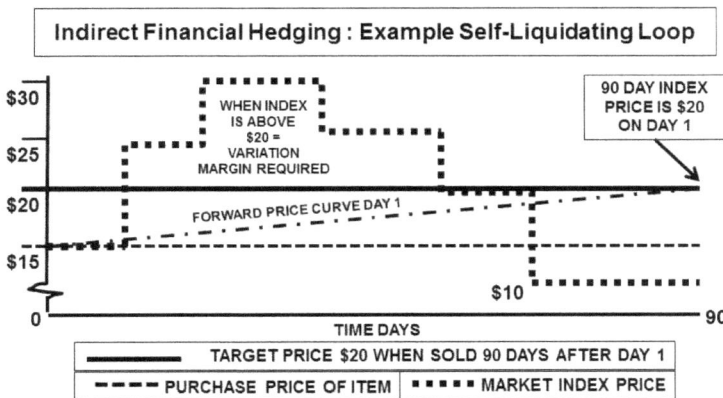

Indirect Financial Hedging : Example Self-Liquidating Loop

DAY 01: BOUGHT ITEM @ $15 & SOLD FUTURE SHORT @ $20
DAY 90: SOLD ITEM @ $10 & BOUGHT FUTURE @ $10 TO COVER SHORT POSITION.
>> LOST $5 ON SALE BUT REALISED $10 ON FUTURE POSITION = PROFIT OF $5 <<

Assessing and Managing Liquidity Risk

Gudni Adalsteinsson, author of *The Liquidity Management Guide* speaking at a Global Association of Risk Professionals (GARP) meeting in London in January 2015, pointed out that major Liquidity Risk events have each had a different genesis. He summarised the situation regarding the technical management challenge posed by Liquidity Risk as follows:

"**Liquidity Risk** has a vague theoretical background; little research has been done.

There is only limited (pertinent) historical data available.

Changing assumptions, drivers and relationships commonly arise, because each major incident is distinct.

The lack of consistent data patterns makes Liquidity Risk difficult to see and measure; hence its very nature does not facilitate learning from past mistakes.

The result is, in the aftermath of each major event, risk professionals must start the analysis with a clean sheet.

Therefore there must be more focus on 'the approach' used in managing liquidity than on attempting to model the risk."

Malcolm T Gladwell, a Canadian journalist and bestselling author, coined the phrase:

"The visionary starts with *a clean sheet of paper* and re-imagines the world."

When addressing the GARP audience, Gudni Adalsteinsson emphasised the need for businesses to incorporate four future orientated elements in a methodology developed for the management of Liquidity Risk; including Extreme Liquidity Risk, which is the risk associated with Black Swan events. These elements are:

A **Liquidity Policy**, underpinned by Liquidity Systems and Procedures.

A **Funding Strategy** supported by a Funding Plan to cover business as usual circumstances.

A **Contingency Funding Plan** designed to identify and to the extent possible to ensure the availability of such funding even in extreme circumstances.

A rolling programme of **Liquidity Stress Testing** that is both future and externally oriented, explicitly considering correlation and systemic market or business connections that could exacerbate the risk.

Liquidity Risk in Financial Institutions

The traditional function of banks is to borrow short term funds from a diverse pool of customers and lend those funds for medium and long term periods to a narrower range of borrowing customers. This model relies upon the relative stability of the short term deposits over the medium to long term, based on the diversity of the depositor portfolio and the presumption that only a relatively small proportion of depositors will withdraw their funds at any one time. That presumption only holds true as long as each and every depositor in the pool believes that the bank will repay his or her deposit on demand, in cash.

The general shortage of retail deposits in recent decades has led banks to additionally source significant portions of the required on-demand deposit funds from wholesale sources, such as other banks, investment funds, pension funds and corporations, thereby increasing the volatility of their deposit base.

The mismatch between the repayable on-demand funding base of a bank on the one hand and its medium to long term loans on the other, has been termed a 'Liquidity Gap'. It is the so called Liquidity Gap that is the main source of Liquidity Risk in financial institutions; in addition to the risks associated with margining described above.

Liquidity Risk in physical businesses arises from different yet not entirely unconnected causes.

Liquidity Risk in Real Businesses

Business enterprises traditionally borrowed medium to long term funds to finance the acquisition or building of infrastructure assets that, in combination with each other, labour and capital, or separately would generate revenue sufficient to meet associated loan repayment commitments. Such assets importantly provide collateral for lenders to the extent that they have a potential resale market or scrap value.

However there is a growing importance of business models that do not require physical assets in order to operate or are based on intangible proprietary assets, such as software or intellectual property, with limited market value. This has led to businesses borrowing medium or long term funds without collateral, on the promise that the business model will continue to be successful; after initially being established with the support of private equity investors, such as Venture Capital Funds.

In addition to margining requirements, if any, short term borrowed funds tend to mainly be used to finance Working Capital. Therefore such cash advances should be self-liquidating, through a cashflow time cycle that is reasonably predictable relative to the entity's revenue generating activities; be those production, manufacturing, transport, trade, wholesale and/or retail.

The total Working Capital locked up in a business, at any one time, is calculated by this formula:

- The value of the inventory the entity holds at cost prices, minus
- The amount it owes the suppliers of that inventory, plus
- The amount owed to the business by its customers, for goods delivered on credit terms.

This formula highlights the fact that an important portion of frozen Working Capital is provided by suppliers. The rest must be covered either by the entity's own funds, or by drawing on repayable-on-demand bank credit lines.

Therefore short term Liquidity Risk assessment and management in real businesses requires focus on two areas;

Firstly the minimisation of Frozen Working Capital requirements, by actively managing inventory levels, credit received from suppliers and credit granted to customers, and

Secondly the strategic management of other sources of short term funding, by assessing the vulnerability of such sources to systemic shocks, ensuring a diversity of sources and developing a flexible contingency funding plan.

Frozen Working Capital Management and the Success Paradox

Frozen Working Capital is a greedy beast that, if allowed to run amok, vacuums up cash and locks it away. This is particularly the case when a business is growing, because increasing sales suck in cash to finance increased inventory on hand and increased given credit. In this way success can weaken a business financially, as it takes on more short term debt to finance increased working capital. Success can mean a weaker, more vulnerable business not a stronger one, hence the 'paradox of success'.

This 'Success Paradox' may be measured by utilising the Cash Flow Cycle formula, which calculates the number of days a business is taking to convert goods into cash. The clock starts when the business pays the cost of acquisition of the goods and stops when the cash from related sales is received.

The formula for calculation of the Cash Flow Cycle, as applied to annual financial statements, is stated as follows:

(Days' Inventory + Days' Sales Outstanding) – Days' Payables

Days' Inventory = Inventory / (Annual Cost of Sales / 365)

Days' Sales Outstanding = Trade Receivables / (Sales / 365)

Days' Payables = Trade Accounts Payable / (Cost of Sales / 365)

Cash Flow Cycle Greed Control Example – Corus Group Plc

Corus Group Plc was formed through the merger of Koninklijke Hoogovens and British Steel on October 6, 1999. The board of directors of this Anglo-Dutch steelmaker accepted a US$7.6 billion takeover bid from Tata Steel of Indian on October 20, 2006, which was consummated in 2007.

Over the period 2002 through 2004, Corus Group Plc evidenced a cash flow cycle of between 64 and 66 days. Hence in 2004 as its sales grew by GB£1.38 billion, the extra cash that became locked up in its Cash Flow Cycle grew by £250 million. This represented some 18% of the sales growth; in other words, for every £5 of additional sales Corus locked away almost £1 in additional working capital.

In 2005 the Corus Cash Flow Cycle averaged 58 days, consequently locking up some GB£1.392 billion in cash throughout the year; details are recorded in the second line of the table printed on the next page.

This analysis provides the basis for action decisions that could release up to GB£912 million from the cycle. The following table also illustrates how that much cash could be released to potentially reduce debt, thereby reduce interest expense and strengthen the Group's financial position.

Working Capital Greed Control

COST OF SALES PER DAY	PAYABLE DAYS	INVENTORY DAYS	RECEIVABLE DAYS [DSO]	CASH CYCLE DAYS	WORKING CAPITAL £ MIO
£24mio	78	82	54	58	1,392
	78	70	54	46	1,104 (288)
	78	82	40	44	1,056 (336)
	90	82	54	46	1,104 (288)
	90	70	40	20	480 (912)

CORUS Group Plc 2005 Example Cash Flow Cycle

Explanatory Notes:

Reducing the amount of Inventory held from 82 days' sales equivalent to 70 days would free up £288 million in cash.

Reducing the number of days of credit afforded to customers from 54 days' sales equivalent to 40 days would free up £336 million in cash.

Increasing the length of the delay after receipt of purchases, before payment is made to suppliers from 78 days' sales equivalent to 90 days would also free up £288 million in cash.

Medium and Long Term Liquidity Risk Management in Real Businesses

Medium to long term Liquidity Risk assessment and management in tangible businesses requires the daily monitoring of cash flow and regular production of cash flow forecasts. Relatively stable businesses should be in a position to develop models to forecast daily cash requirements fairly accurately.

Cashflow forecasts (daily for up to a month ahead then weekly) should consist of five sub-sections namely;

- Contracted (certain) cash flows in and out per period
- Non-contracted (estimated) cash flows in and out per period
- Net certain plus or minus estimated cash surplus or deficit before management action
- Balance per period after management action
- Result of Stress Testing applied to the surplus or deficit before management action

Infrastructure Projects – Staged Payment Commitments

Any medium or long term finance arrangement that is to initially be drawn down in tranches, for example by making progress payments to a building developer, must be carefully constructed. The borrowing entity's reliance on the lender to supply funds in future periods makes it vulnerable to the risk that the lender may be unable to provide the agreed loan tranches at some point before the project has been completed.

In such a case incurring the marginal extra expense of having the full amount of the contracted loan immediately paid into an escrow account, independently held on behalf of both lender and borrower, may be an acceptable way to limit the risk.

Chapter 4

Operational Risk

Operational Risk has two faces; an internal impact face and an external impact face. This chapter will cover the external impact face.

A recent GARP Operational Risk report quoted the following definition:

"Operational risk is the risk of loss resulting from inadequate or failed processes or systems, human factors or external events."

Therefore there are four main causes of operational risk that are identified in standard operational risk definitions namely inadequacies or failures due to;
- people (human factors),
- processes,
- systems or
- external events.

Unfortunately the possible impact of external events is often ignored because operational risk assessment and management is inward focussed in many cases. People naturally prefer to manage what they can see and control, however it is operational risk driven by external events that is most likely to seriously damage a business entity.

As suppliers, supply-chains and customers have become more dispersed across the globe the ripple effect of a Black Swan event can significantly affect the survival and growth prospects of a business whether or not it is geographically proximate.

Margaret Rouse, noted in a post on Whatis.com that "in 1972 Edward Lorenz, a meteorologist, explained Chaos Theory by posing the rhetorical question; 'Does the Flap of a Butterfly's Wings in Brazil set off a Tornado in Texas?'

The example of such a small system as a butterfly being responsible for creating such a large and distant system as a tornado in Texas illustrates the impossibility of making predictions for complex systems; despite the fact that these are determined by underlying conditions, precisely what those conditions are can never be sufficiently articulated to allow long-range predictions."

Accordingly Chaos Theory postulates that:

'A small change near the beginning of a series of physical cause-and-effect actions will change the outcome significantly and unpredictably'.

Hence it is no longer sufficient to simply control those operational activities within an organisation. Attention must be given to the activities, locations, environments, policies and risk management methods of all associated suppliers, logistics providers, storage companies and customers.

Wherever a business has a connection that connection has the potential to transmit the fallout or opportunity from an event to which the entity in question is not otherwise connected.

Looking back along every connection chain to identify risks is therefore a vital Operational Risk management activity.

The Risk that almost destroyed Ericsson in March 2000

Sunil Chopra and ManMohan S. Sodhi, in an article for the MIT Sloan Management Review titled *Managing Risk to Avoid Supply-Chain Breakdown* in October 2004 wrote:

"On March 17, 2000, lightning hit a power line in Albuquerque, New Mexico, USA. The strike caused a massive surge in the surrounding electrical grid, which in turn started a fire at a local plant owned by Royal Philips Electronics, N.V., damaging millions of microchips.

Scandinavian mobile-phone manufacturer Nokia Corp., a major customer of the plant, almost immediately began switching its chip orders to other Philips plants, as well as to other Japanese and American suppliers. Thanks to its multiple-supplier strategy and responsiveness, Nokia's production suffered little during the (subsequent) crisis.

In contrast, Telefon AB L.M. Ericsson, another mobile-phone customer of the Philips plant, employed a single-sourcing policy. As a result, when the Philips plant shut down after the fire, Ericsson had no other source of microchips, which disrupted production for months. (Through the first quarter after the fire Ericsson lost US$500 million.) Ericsson has since implemented new processes and tools for preventing such scenarios.

These two dramatically different outcomes from one event, demonstrate the importance of proactively managing supply-chain risk. Supply-chain problems result from natural disasters, labour disputes, supplier bankruptcy, acts of war and terrorism, and other causes. They can seriously disrupt or delay material, information and cash flows, any of which can damage sales (and/or) increase costs. Broadly categorised, potential supply-chain risks include delays, disruptions, forecast inaccuracies, systems breakdowns, intellectual property breaches, procurement failures, inventory problems and capacity issues."

Closer scrutiny of the Ericsson case by Karamjeet Paul recently revealed that Ericsson and other customers were contacted by Philips immediately after the initial damage had been assessed. At that time Philips indicated it would suffer a one week delay in deliveries of chips ordered. In the case of Ericsson a purchasing administrator was advised and the details of the incident and prospective delay – then thought to be of little consequence – were not widely communicated within the business.

Two weeks later Philips advised restarting production in Albuquerque would be further delayed 'a few weeks'. This updated time-line was again not disseminated within Ericsson as the receiver did not understand the repercussions. The restart of production was in fact delayed several months. When Ericsson senior management eventually became aware of the seriousness of the situation it was too late to source the chips elsewhere since no other manufacturing facility had any spare capacity available. As a result Ericsson was not able to field a competitive product during the high consumer demand 'holiday season'.

The consequence was the realisation of a net loss of some US$2.3 billion by year end. Moreover, six months after the fire Ericsson's market share had fallen from 12% to 9%. A year later Ericsson announced its withdrawal from cell phone production via a 50/50 joint venture established with Sony.

The losses suffered by Philips due to the fire were covered by insurance but that was not so in the case of losses suffered by its customers.

This is a good example of a micro- Black Swan or single-victim high-impact unique event having unpredictable consequences for connected parties.

Although Ericsson suffered major losses its better prepared competitor, which was quicker to act and secure alternative sources of microchips, benefitted handsomely from its difficulties. Nokia's market share increased from 27% to 30% within six months of the fire; since it was able to meet the market demand that would otherwise have been won by Ericsson.

Toyota profit slides on Japan earthquake disruption

On May 11, 2011 Associated Press reported:

"Toyota is expected to lose its spot as the world's top-selling carmaker to General Motors this year because of the disruption to its output.

Toyota's quarterly profit crumbled more than 75% after the March 11th earthquake and tsunami wiped out parts suppliers in north-eastern Japan, severely disrupting car production.

Toyota president Akio Toyoda said the company was still missing about 30 types of parts, although that was an improvement from the 150 it had lacked before. Toyota hopes to be producing at 70% of its pre-quake levels by June."

Worst Thai Floods in 50 Years hit Toyota Supply Chain

Wikipedia under the title *2011 Thailand Floods* records:

"Severe flooding occurred during the 2011 monsoon season in Thailand. Beginning at the end of July triggered by the landfall of Tropical Storm Nock-ten, flooding soon spread through the provinces of Northern, North-eastern and Central Thailand along the Mekong and Chao Phraya river basins. In October floodwaters reached the mouth of the Chao Phraya and inundated parts of the capital city of Bangkok."

The World Bank considered that the 2011 Thai floods were, at the time, the world's fourth most costly disaster; surpassed only by the 2011 earthquake and tsunami in Japan, the 1995 Kobe earthquake and Hurricane Katrina in 2005.

These two 2011 macro- Black Swan events had repercussions well beyond the borders of the countries where they occurred; manufacturing supply chains were disrupted as were global financial markets. Toyota suffered supply chain disruption as a result of both disasters, and the consequent electricity shortages in Japan caused by the shutting down of the country's nuclear power stations. However Bloomberg reported that other globally significant manufacturers were also negatively affected, for example:

Apple Inc reported that Thailand's worst floods in half a century delayed supply of components used in Mac computers.

Western Digital Corporation, the world's largest maker of hard-disk drives, warned its production would not return to normal for months.

Honda Motor Co., Nissan Motor Co. and Toyota were reported to have lost an aggregate of 6,000 units of production daily while their plants in Thailand were closed. Most cars made in Thailand are exported to markets from Australia to Europe and Mexico.

General Motors Co. and Ford Motor Co. also had to suspend production in their Thai manufacturing hubs.

A Toyota affiliate Aisin Seiki Co.'s aluminium die-cast factory in central Thailand had to evacuate the plant's 1,500 workers on October 18.

Flooding disrupted Nikon Corporation's electronics production. Nikon is the world's second-largest maker of cameras with interchangeable lenses.

Sony Corporation, Japan's largest exporter of consumer electronics, delayed the release of some cameras and headphones due to Thai manufacturing disruptions. The company was seeking an alternative production base for cameras after flooding partially damaged its plant in Ayutthaya, where almost all of its high-end cameras were produced.

Canon Incorporated, the world's largest producer of cameras, stopped production at two factories in Ayutthaya, which is a city situated 80 kilometres north of Bangkok. Ayutthaya is a UNESCO designated world heritage site.

Five Hitachi Ltd plants suspended production of electronic and metal components, including parts for car brakes and compressors for refrigerators.

Toshiba Corporation, Japan's largest maker of memory chips, halted production at nine factories that made products including hard-disk drives, solid state drives, chips and household electronics.

Managing Operational Risk

Operational risk by its nature occurs across a series of connected events; as such it encompasses a variety of risk types, some of which are insurable, others avoidable by means of adopting standards and procedures. Some elements of risk can be limited by ensuring involved employees have adequate experience and training, others by diversifying sources or means of transport for example. Legal risks can be limited by the proper drafting of contracts under guidance from or by suitably qualified and experienced lawyers.

Operational risk is inherent in any physical transaction from the time the deal is struck or the purchase order placed until the correct quantity and quality of the subject good or service is delivered to the buyer.

Most physical transactions are complex, involving several parties, countries and modes of transport. It is unusual for any two transactions, even those within a series of similar transactions, to proceed from initiation to completion in exactly the same way. This is one of the most significant ways in which physical transactions differ from pure financial transactions. It is the difference that requires the operational risk manager to have the ability to solve practical problems as they arise, usually without notice and at times without precedent. It requires a flexible 'can do' attitude and a solution finding or solution creating approach. Essential is an in-depth knowledge of the appropriate market, supply-chain and participants, which can only be gained through experience or apprenticeship to a master of the art and practice.

Those operational risks the control of which is within the power of the owners or managers of a business, amongst others, are covered in Chapter 9.

External Event Driven Operational Risk Management

Limiting Supply-Chain Related Damage

There are a number of preparatory steps that can be taken to ensure that a business is capable of withstanding a supply-chain disruption caused by an unanticipated and un-insurable remote event.

- Identify all key inputs that are provided by third parties for the manufacturing or service provision processes of the business.
- Draw a web diagram linking the business back along each supply-chain to each third party.
- Extend each supply chain beyond each direct third party supplier to reveal each party's external supplier connections.
- Identify the geographic location of every relevant supplier manufacturing or service providing facility.
- Obtain from each direct third party supplier details of its plans to maintain supply provision should its main facility be incapacitated.
- Such plans should cover both physical and cyber-related dangers; such as unauthorised access to control and other systems and data theft. These plans must be reviewed and updated regularly. In cases when third parties do not wish to disclose some details it should be possible to agree that an independent organisation will be contracted to review such plans and report on their likely effectiveness.

- Identify suitable alternative supply sources for all inputs normally obtained from third parties and arrange diversity of supply where practicable.

Web or Spider Diagram Example

A UK based manufacturer of a range of 'high-end' branded bicycles, may begin describing its potential exposure to connected yet remote external risks by compiling a table like the example on the next page:

Inputs for manufacturing	Parts bought from specialist suppliers	Accessories by others	Distribution connections
Sheets of carbon fibre cloth sourced from one supplier based in Dusseldorf, Germany	Saddles supplied by Selle Italia, based in Asolo, near Treviso in Italy	Pumps and repair kits WIDELY AVAILABLE	Road transport in the UK utilising various providers.
Epoxy sourced from two 'formulators' based in Connecticut USA and Scotland UK respectively	Safari Bikes Ltd Ludhiana Punjab India Handlebars & Hubs	Reflective decals WIDELY AVAILABLE	Road transport in mainland Europe and Ireland using various providers crossing via ferry from various ports and the Channel Tunnel shuttle.
Electricity supplied via the national grid by a major utility.	Supplier 3 Wheels Tires and inner tubes	Lights WIDELY AVAILABLE	Urgent and over-seas (e.g. Middle East, Australia, the USA and LatAm) via air freight.
Water supplied by the regional water company.	Supplier 4 Pedals & Chains	Bells WIDELY AVAILABLE	Online sales channel provided but most sales via appointed specialist distrib-utors able to advise potential customers.
Aluminium supplied by ELVAL based in Greece, near the Tanagra Airport in the Oinofyta city area, north of Ath-ens and the All.co Group factory in Tuscany, Italy.	Supplier 5 Brake assemblies and gears		

The Operational Risk Executive would then draft a Supplier Connections Spider Diagram as illustrated by the examples that appear on the following two pages.

NORTHERN EUROPE

CARBON FIBRE
CLOTH FROM
DUSSELDORF
GERMANY

*Transport disruption
(protests or strikes)*

EPOXY FROM
SCOTLAND UK

Weather delays

USA — EAST COAST

EPOXY
FROM CT USA

*Severe winter
storms
Transport delays
Export regulation
changes*

UK ELECTRICITY

UK
BICYCLE
MAKER

UK WATER

SOUTHERN EUROPE

ALUMINIUM FROM
OINOFYTA, GREECE

ALUMINIUM FROM
TUSCANY, ITALY

SADDLES
FROM ASOLO
TREVISO, ITALY

*All in earthquake
zones*

PUNJAB — INDIA

HANDLEBARS
& HUBS
FROM LUDHIANA
PUNJAB, INDIA

*Civil strife / strikes
War with Pakistan
(situated close
to the border)
Natural disasters
Infrastructure failures*

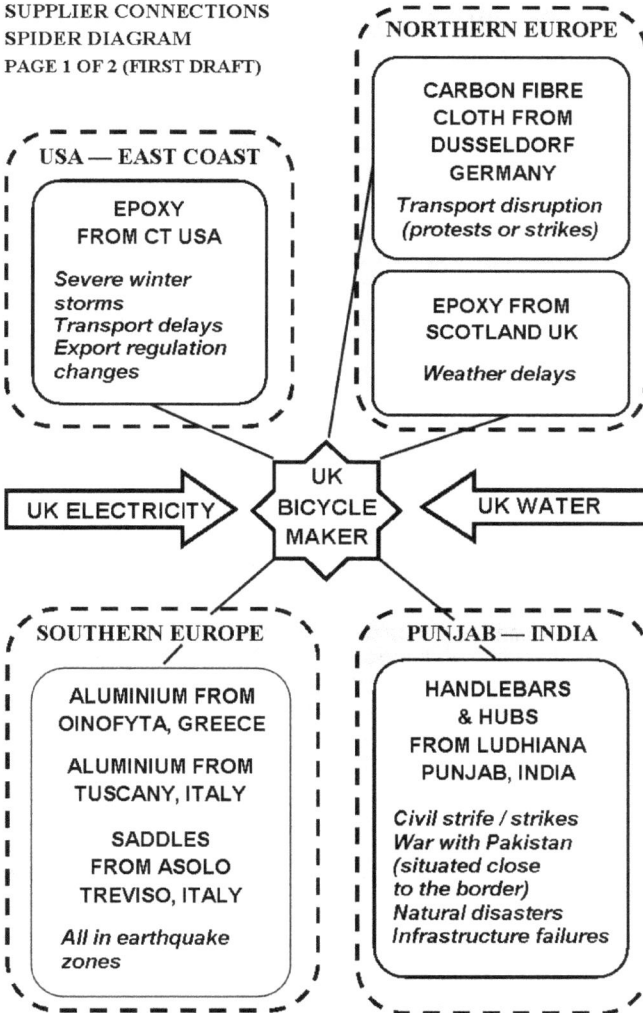

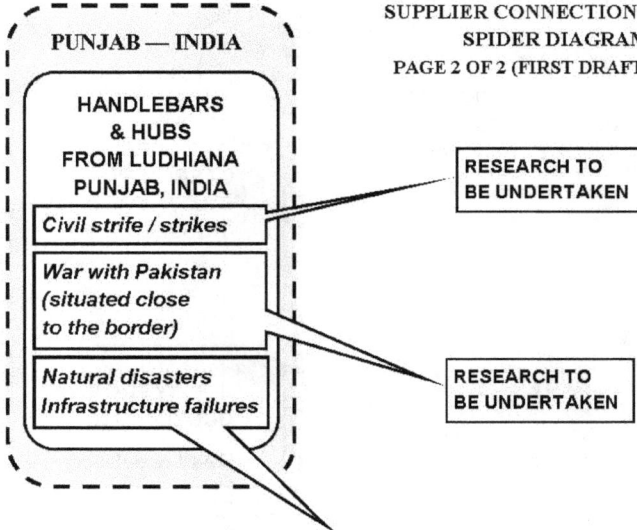

PUNJAB — INDIA

HANDLEBARS
& HUBS
FROM LUDHIANA
PUNJAB, INDIA

Civil strife / strikes

*War with Pakistan
(situated close
to the border)*

*Natural disasters
Infrastructure failures*

RESEARCH TO
BE UNDERTAKEN

RESEARCH TO
BE UNDERTAKEN

FAILURE OF THE PUBLIC POWER GRID

IF THE LOCAL AND/OR REGIONAL ELECTRICITY SUPPLY
WERE TO FAIL FOR AN EXTENDED PERIOD PRODUCTION
WOULD BE HALTED. TO AVOID THIS THE FOLLOWING
MEASURES ARE IN PLACE:

- A COMBINATION OF ONSITE INSTALLED SOLAR, WIND,
  BATTERIES AND BIOGAS PROVIDES THE FACTORY WITH
  30% OF ITS NORMAL POWER REQUIRED
- A STANDBY DIESEL GENERATOR CAN PROVIDE ENOUGH
  ADDITIONAL POWER TO MAINTAIN PRODUCTION

*These precautions appear to be adequate in respect of
power, provided access to diesel for the generator is
reasonably assured. Note: Check diesel supply
contingency plans.*

In this way a business can identify the remote regions, suppliers and suppliers-to-those-suppliers that must be continuously monitored in order to identify any possible supply-chain disruption at the earliest possible moment.

The final step in this process is to establish a protocol for immediate and effective communication of any risks identified, and to allocate responsibility for deciding and taking corrective action.

Chapter 5

Concentration & Correlation Risk

Frequently Hidden – Often Deadly

Correlation is a concept widely applied in the financial sector where institutions own and manage portfolios of and/or trade bonds, stocks (shares) and derivatives (collectively known as 'securities').

Investopedia on its website – www.investopedia.com - explains correlation as follows:

> "In the world of finance, correlation is a statistical measure of how two securities move in relation to each other. Correlations are used in advanced portfolio management.
>
> Correlation is computed into what is known as the correlation coefficient, which ranges between -1 and +1. Perfect positive correlation (a correlation coefficient of +1) implies that as one security moves, either up or down (in value), the other security will move in lockstep, in the same direction. Alternatively, perfect negative correlation means that if one security moves in either direction the security that is perfectly negatively correlated will move in the opposite direction. If the correlation is 0, the movements of the securities (relative to each other) are said to have no correlation; they are completely random."

A portfolio is a group of assets of a similar class, hence generally in this sense a physical enterprises' only portfolio of assets is 'receivable accounts'; in other words trade debtors. Therefore in the world occupied by physical businesses the purely financial concept of correlation has limited useful applicability.

Receivable accounts portfolio management is discussed fully in *Global Credit Management – An Executive Summary* published by John Wiley & Sons.

In all other respects the concept of Correlation Risk is most useful to real businesses when employed in consort with the concept of Concentration Risk.

As stated in the previous chapter, Corus Group Plc was formed through the merger of Koninklijke Hoogovens and British Steel on October 6, 1999. The board of directors of this Anglo-Dutch steelmaker accepted a US$7.6 billion takeover bid from Tata Steel of Indian on October 20, 2006, which was consummated in 2007.

An analysis of the 2004 Annual Financial Report of Corus Group reveals that its sales revenue during that year was derived from the following industry groups:

- 30% Construction
- 16% Automotive
- 15% Packaging
- 14% Mechanical Engineering
- 13% Metal Goods
- 12% Other

It is clear that in 2004 Corus had Concentration Risk in respect of its revenue stream; specifically it was excessively reliant on revenues derived from sales to the construction sector.

To make matters worse, the success or otherwise of the participant businesses in the construction sector of most economies is positively correlated. When the sector is booming, all participants see turnover and profits rise but when the 'bubble bursts' all suffer a reversal of fortunes.

This example illustrates the value of identifying and tracking concentrations within a physical business. Corus was not in the construction industry sector, it was in iron and steel, but through the concentration of its revenue in the construction sector it was additionally exposed to the risks faced by that sector.

As well as 'revenue by industry sector', concentrations can be identified in several aspects of business, for example:

- Revenue by buyer country or region
- Material supplies by country or region
- Trade receivables by customer and/or customer risk rating group
- Revenue by customer
- Relative quantity of certain types of purchases by supplier
- Category of product by customer
- Deposits placed with or loans and/or guarantees from individual banks

Identifying and regularly tracking any significant concentrations will arm executives with the necessary information to act effectively when something positive or negative that affects a particular concentration class occurs.

Geographic Concentration and Correlation Risk Example

According to Demitrios Kalogeropoulos writing in *The Motley Fool* blog on April 6, 2015;

"Costco operates about 700 warehouses around the world, including in huge international economies such as Japan, the United Kingdom, and Mexico. But more than 70% of its sales come from the United States. And within the U.S. a whopping 32% of Costco's revenue is generated in California.

The Golden State has 'a larger percentage of higher volume warehouses as compared to our other domestic markets,' Costco warned. That's important because 'any substantial slowing in these operations' would have an outsized effect on the company's overall results. In other words, Costco is heavily exposed to the strength -- or weakness -- of the California market."

This comment clearly suggests that Costco's future viability is closely correlated with the future strength or weakness of the Californian market, providing an example of the value of undertaking research to uncover concentrations within a business.

Although this suggested correlation is not supported by a precise number (coefficient) that is the result of the manipulation of a data-based mathematical model, it is logical. Therefore it is reasonable to believe that the connection is worthy of surveillance by any organisation that identifies Costco as a major customer or supplier.

Hence in the context of any physical business it is relatively easy to identify with certainty the exposure concentrations that exist but the factors or variables with which such concentrations may be correlated must be deduced.

It is emphasised that the factors or variables with which concentrations may be correlated must be deduced employing logic, experience, imagination and any relevant data that may exist.

Chapter 6

Lack of Flexibility and Agility

In 2013 Nokia lost its status as the industry leader having fallen in smart-phone ranking to 10, from number 1 in 2011. This led to the sale of its Devices and Services business to Microsoft in April 2014.

In May 2013, Julian Birkinshaw (Professor of Strategic and International Management at London Business School) published an article in which he analysed the reason why successful companies like Nokia, that are aware of the changes going on around them, own leading-edge technology and employ expert marketers, "nevertheless fail to convert awareness into action".

Birkinshaw's conclusion is that such companies lack "the capacity to change in a decisive and committed way." He continues:

> "The failure of big companies to adapt to changing circumstances is one of the fundamental puzzles in the world of business. Occasionally, a genuinely 'disruptive' technology, such as digital imaging, comes along and wipes out an entire industry. But usually the sources of failure are more prosaic and avoidable — a failure to implement technologies that have already been developed, an arrogant disregard for changing customer demands, or a complacent attitude towards new competitors."

It is clear that the inability to flex an organisation in order to change quickly enough to catch each shift in its market, potentially threatens its survival. The increasingly potent and very real threat posed by Ignored External Change is a risk that hovers ever present, menacing every business.

The Enemies of Agility – Ignored External Change

Dealing with the dangerous inertia that all too soon becomes the norm in most successful businesses requires the identification of the 'enemies of agility'. Birkinshaw identifies five in his article:

"**Ossified management processes**: Things get done in big firms through management processes — budgeting and planning, performance management, and succession planning. These processes create simplicity and order, but they also become entrenched and self-reinforcing.

Old and narrow metrics: What gets measured gets done, but we don't refresh our choices of measures frequently enough, and we end up with massive blind spots.

A disenfranchised front line: The first insights into changes in your business environment come from the people on the 'front line' — salespeople, developers working with third parties, purchasing managers, but their voice — if it is raised at all — typically gets drowned out among all the others clamouring for executive attention.

Lack of diversity: Nokia's top executives were all Fins of similar age and background, and this surely hampered their ability to make sense of their changing business environment.

Intolerance of failure: The bigger and more successful a firm becomes, the more risk-averse it becomes. Executives say they want innovative new products and services, but they expect them all to succeed; needless to say, this attitude breeds caution and rigidity."

Although these enemies of agility are often identified in the aftermath of the failure of a once successful, seemingly unassailable, enterprise debilitated by its lack of ability to change, the costly lessons taught by such examples as Nokia and Kodak are widely ignored.

Professor Birkinshaw, fellow academics and consultants are able to supply generalised solutions, through articles such as the one quoted above, which is available on the website www.managementexchange.com.

However an organisation will only become flexible and agile if its leadership;

- Embraces the need to regularly mentally step outside the corporate environment and consider how its customers could avail of the utility it provides differently,
- Genuinely listens to its employees, customers and consultants, and
- Abandons the notion of 'sacred cows' so that no aspect of the business is exempt from change.

Nadya Zhexembayeva in her TEDx Talk *To Hold On, Let Go*, in April 2015 (available at: https://youtu.be/f4kySpcdvFg) made the following points, among several others:

"The fast-moving roller-coaster economy we live in today makes (surviving) increasingly difficult. Just as we handle one crisis, another looms around the corner. How can we (endure) — and even thrive?

The answer is: We must consistently remake who we are, what we offer, and how we deliver our offerings to the world. Put it simply, we must reinvent.

What you may not have heard before is this: Today, the frequency with which our reinvention must take place is staggering. Essentially, we must become a new company every three years.

Sustainability (in the sense of keeping things the way they are now) doesn't drive life. Change does.

Nothing in the world *holds on*.

So, if *holding on* and *locking down* don't work, what can we do? How do companies survive? How can we sustain?

The real secret of sustainability is simple: *take the essence of what you are, and let go of everything else.* It is that essential core that you need to propel forward, reinventing yourself vigorously over and over again, with a rapidity that is (shocking).

Instead of desperately trying to stay in business by all means possible, it is time for you to get out of business — and get into a newer one.

The business you are in today (will) not be the business you'll be in 3 years from now. By then, you (will be) either entering your new business or you (will be) on the way to extinction; *period.*

So, forget 'built to last'. Build to reinvent."

Nevertheless it is difficult to imagine any business transforming itself in the way required if the sentiments expressed by Rowan Gibson, et alia, in *Rethinking the Future* represent a widespread malaise:

"If you draw an organisation pyramid with senior management at the top, you need to ask the question: Where in the pyramid do you find the least genetic diversity when it comes to thinking in radically different ways about the future of an industry? And where in that pyramid do you find managers who have most of their emotional equity invested in the past? It's at the top. Then you ask: Whom do we give the primary responsibility for strategy setting and direction? The same guys; no wonder we don't receive anything very creative out."

"Most importantly, it should be recognised that the existing hierarchy in most organisations is a hierarchy of experience and not a hierarchy of imagination. There is a big difference between experience and imagination. Never has experience been worth less, and never has imagination been more central to future success."

Fortunately there are examples of organisations that have changed and are successful; thereby showing that Ignored External Change risk can be overcome. The next section presents some examples and suggested risk management interventions.

The Agents of Agility

It has been written that "the Industrial Age was rules-based leading to procedures; on the other hand the Information Age is based on principles leading to creativity and innovation. Therefore there is now a need for real-time, dynamic, spontaneous, even instantaneous, tactical decision making".

This notion is fully discussed by George Kobak in his March 10, 2015 article titled *Can Corporate Tactical Planning Survive in the Information Age?*

Empowerment and Organisation Structure

In order to respond dynamically in real-time to customer needs and market changes, every employee must be equipped to be a leader. This particularly applies to those working in the front line, in the so called 'value zone'; that is the space where value is created at the interface with customers. They must be supported in two ways that require traditional management styles to change radically, namely:

- They must be provided with details of the Purpose of their jobs (how their jobs help to make the world a better place), the values of the business (in order of importance so they can know which value to favour should a decision cause conflict between the ideals) and the ultimate future state the organisation aims to achieve.

Daniel H Pink in *Drive* stated "Human beings have an innate inner drive to be autonomous, self-determined, and connected to one another; when that drive is liberated, people achieve more and live richer lives." In other words, if employees at all levels are empowered with knowledge of the purpose, values/ideals, ultimate aim and current economic state of the organisation they can customise and flex their activities and actions to automatically respond to changes in customer and task demands. In this way they can also provide useful signals to a supportive leadership cadre as to what is changing and what needs to be changed.

- Secondly they must be supported by an inverted organisation structure, such as that developed by Vineet Nayar CEO of HCL Technologies, and described by Gary Hamel in *What Matters Now*.

  Nayar explained that "The old (management) processes (in HCLT) were focussed on running the business. We needed new processes that were focussed on changing the business." As an example, he subsequently determined that "Powerful staff departments, such as HR and Finance, often seem more interested in enforcing blanket policies than in making life easier to employees. Recognising this, Vineet started querying frontline employees: 'What have the enabling functions done to help you create value in the value zone?' His question was usually met with silence, and a quizzical look. When it came to interaction with these functions, most employees felt like supplicants, a situation that was hardly empowering. The (HCLT) Solution: a web-based *Smart Service Desk* where any employee could open a 'service ticket' if they had a complaint with an internal staff group. A ticket could only be closed by the employee concerned; if not closed promptly it would be escalated. In the first month 30,000 tickets were issued." This and other revolutionary changes such as an Employees First Customers Second (EFCS) policy, introduced by Vineet Nayar had a dramatically positive impact on the success of HCLT.

Imagination and Innovation

Klaus Schwab, Founder & Executive Chair of World Economic Forum wrote on February 19, 2015:

"Whatever the changes (in future), almost all of them will present a challenge. As new technologies make old jobs obsolete, for example, every person will have to make sure they are equipped with the skills needed for this new era of 'talentism' – where human imagination and innovation are the driving forces behind economies, as opposed to capital or natural resources."

A report by Accenture Strategy titled *The Future-Ready Organisation - Reinventing Work in ASEAN* published in 2014 noted that these driving forces (imagination and innovation) neatly dovetail with the aspirations of the majority of people new to or entering the work force. In part the report states:

"Future workplaces must be more flexible, and the jobs they offer more engaging to retain talent.

Generation Y workers have a strong desire to prove their abilities. 'It's not about the money... Give me an opportunity: I will deliver.' They want more responsibility.

Employers will need to take into account millennials' need for a sense of purpose in their work and clearly illustrate how this work has a positive social impact. In addition, employees of the future workforce will want to play a more active role in creating their own job descriptions and designing career paths.

Workers will hold 20 to 30 jobs over the course of five to six careers, which could include part-time stints, and working as a contractor. These shifts challenge traditions and beliefs about the value or need for hierarchy, job titles and promotions, and even salary progression.

Learning and development will be treated as a lifelong journey and an important part of most employers' value proposition. Employers will offer capability development options that incorporate massive open online courses (MOOCs) and gamification strategies. Many companies will also adopt game-based work practices to encourage workplace behaviours such as goal-setting in their younger employees with their different expectations of work and digital fluency. A veteran Singapore government official is convinced that 'one of the best ways to be creative and to be innovative is to *gamify* the work that we do' to inject an element of play into work activities."

Harnessing the collective ideas of employees in order to meet the challenges of social, demographic, technological and customer expectation changes is difficult to prioritise because failure to do so is not reported. However if this is not achieved the danger is that a whole business could be lost as new business models arise.

Freelancing and Sharing Business Resources (SBR)

Peer to peer; business to business sharing of resources is a trend that is an important part of the future that is 'just not very evenly distributed' in 2015. However as such it is providing those businesses that have already embraced the concept with important competitive advantages.

Robert Vaughan, writing in an article titled *The Sharing Company*, published by PWC in October 2014 chronicled this development as follows:

"The less reported trend emerging from the sharing economy, (which is) just beginning to attract media attention, probably presents a larger opportunity than (Airbnb type) 'consumer sharing'.

It is the open sharing of resources among businesses: peer-to-peer enterprise exchange. In just a few years of activity, it has become clear that the unfettered exchange of otherwise unused major assets, including physical space and industrial equipment, allows a sharing company to operate more efficiently than its non-sharing rivals.

Companies that go further still, wholeheartedly embracing the sharing of less tangible assets, may benefit from a different sort of change, one involving their culture, which builds new types of connections with, and sensitivity to, the world outside. By tearing down the walls and airing their secrets — whether they are 'we have underutilised talent' or 'we have great know-how but aren't sure how to turn it into something people want to buy' — these companies can both improve their own bottom line and contribute to the collective good."

Concurrently **freelance working** among professionals of all types has been growing steadily since 2013, when the merged Elance and oDesk web based market place brokered US$750 million worth of work. This development has important implications for the search for risk reducing and risk management flexibility by both businesses and individuals. Robert Vaughan also covers this point in the mentioned article:

"Platforms (such as oDesk) allow firms to recruit a flexible, task-oriented workforce without worrying about how to keep them busy during a downturn. They are also likely to draw more talented people, who can now gain the kinds of creative opportunities at multiple companies that are typically available only to short-term contractors, while retaining the substantial benefits that accrue to valued staffers with a single employer. This best-of-both-worlds approach could come to be seen as the most enviable way to work."

Change and Business in the Future

This chapter closes with a quotation from the website of the Institute for Global Futures, the Business Futures page, which can be accessed via www.globalfuturist.com:

"Complex and real-time changes will become the norm for business in the 21st century. At the same time we forecast going back to the future. Business leaders need to develop a capacity to envision future opportunities as well as challenges. The short term focus that grips many organisations misses rich opportunities for future success.

There are vast changes yet to come that will frustrate but change every aspect of business. Developing the capacity as a leader to become Future Smart, to learn to anticipate future trends and change may well become the key skill for survival.

Technology will be the major enabling force for business in the future, transforming supply chains, value nets, business models, work-styles and opening up new global markets for expansion.

The full integration of technology into business will transform commerce, just as society is being altered. This is the first wave of digital global electronic economics, a new model. The convergence of artificial intelligence, data mining, the next Internet, supply chain engineering, business process change and wireless eBusiness will create both disruptions and opportunities."

It is worth repeating that changes will "create both disruptions and opportunities" in order to emphasise that ineffective business risk assessment and management is dangerous in both the sense of missed opportunities and failure to avoid losses.

RISK TOOLS FOR UNKNOWN UNKNOWNS

Described in this section are the risk assessment and management tools available to those executives who will be responsible for the ongoing viability of a physical business when a Black Swan event strikes.

Chapter 7

Courage - Decisions without Data

If you can't hide behind numbers, how can you find the courage to make a decision?

We all prefer to rely on numbers (usually data organised on an Excel spreadsheet) when making significant decisions. Numbers are so reassuring, so precise, they 'add up' and one can check their veracity against other numbers; just to be certain of the supporting grounds. What is more, since they represent real events that occurred in the past, even if they are projections based on those real events they are 'solid', originated in reality.

However as Karamjeet Paul pointed out in his ground-breaking text *Managing Extreme Financial Risk*:

> "***If it seems too good to be true, then it probably is*** used to be the old mantra.
>
> Now, something too good to be true (but supported by a mathematical model) is often mistakenly assumed to be the result of a super-intelligent, complex quant analysis.
>
> Despite all the complexities (of the products being traded), shouldn't sound human judgement have said something about AIG Financial Products (Division) raking in so much money (in 2007-8) that they didn't know what to do with it?"

On September 16, 2008 the Wall Street Journal reported: "The U.S. government seized control of American International Group Inc. (AIG) -- one of the world's biggest insurers -- in an $85 billion deal that signalled the intensity of its concerns about the danger a collapse could pose to the financial system."

Therefore, in this instance alone, blind faith in mathematical models cost U.S. Tax Payers $85 billion.

In summary; we cannot rely on numbers.

Therefore, on what basis can decisions be made and defended?

The answer is, by employing Noitanigami – it's like Mojo only more powerful.

Imagining the Future

When making a decision it is common to mentally play forward the chain of events that one anticipates will occur as a direct result of implementation of that decision. An experienced decision maker would include consideration of what could go wrong and threaten the occurrence of an unexpected outcome. Naturally in anticipating possible unexpected outcomes one would be likely to anticipate what remedial action involved parties could employ. Some remedies imagined would involve nuancing the decision, perhaps purchasing insurance, amending or adding a contract clause, or requiring other parties to provide collateral, such as guarantees.

A Fictional Illustration:
A Business Decision Thought Process

Approval of a contract to supply a Buyer based in Shanghai, with purchased Dressage Saddles designed and handmade in England, United Kingdom.

Research undertaken during the normal due diligence process has confirmed that neither Saddlemakers (the manufacturer) nor the Shanghai Buyer or the respective controlling parties appear on OFAC's Specially Designated Nationals List or the Bank of England – Consolidated List of Financial Sanction Targets. Furthermore Dressage Saddles are not restricted export goods.

It is noted that the saddles have been designed through application of research and development, with the support of many of the world's leading international riders and trainers, over 30 years.

Risks considered by the Decision Maker (DM) include:

- As a consequence of dealing with Saddlemakers and/or the Buyer the company could be charged with aiding money laundering or terrorist financing offences.
  - o This risk is limited by the standing due diligence process, which has been completed.
- The manufacturer may not provide the number or quality of saddles promised. This risk is characterised as Supplier Performance Risk.
  - o Manufacturer has operated successfully for 30 years and has a good reputation for quality and on time delivery; however this is a key risk since the related sales contract includes a penalty clause relating to failure to deliver and/or quality issues.
  - o After visiting the manufacturer to understand its managements' plans to cope with the additional volume demands and associated working capital finance requirements, the DM accepts that its contingency plans are likely to be adequate. The manufacturer's profit margin and cash flow cycle will support volume growth, there is spare capacity that can be brought online quickly and additional skilled craft workers are being trained.
- The product may not find a market at the target price level and/or adequate volume demand. This is an aspect of Buyer Performance Risk.
  - o The Buyer has undertaken extensive market research having initially discovered the Heilan International Equestrian Club, situated in XinQiao, a 'small' city not far from Shanghai, in Jiangsu Province, China. Previously the DM had no idea a dressage mecca existed in China. The Buyer advised that; "Heilan International Equestrian Club has been busy importing horses from Europe and the United States,

constructing a jaw-dropping facility and training a legion of riders. The highlight of Heilan's Equestrian programme is the weekly sold-out riding exhibition, narrated in Mandarin. Performed every Saturday evening with mid-week encore performances during the high season, it features four main carousel segments that form the heart of the show, presenting groups of choreographed dressage horses and riders." This was confirmed in a report published by Dressage Today in June 2012 and video clips appearing on YouTube.

- o Nothing is certain in China but a report in 2013 noting that the dressage team of Xinjiang province was preparing in Beijing for the qualifiers to the 12th National Games in Liaoning encouraged the DM to believe that the popularity of dressage had begun to spread beyond the Heilan establishment. The National Games hold almost the same significance as the Olympic Games in China. Hence the opportunity to sell acceptable volumes seemed to exist with sufficient certainty.
- o According to the contract the Buyer is obligated to pay for the saddles it receives in China whether or not they are subsequently sold, so the internal market risk would be borne by the Buyer.
- Import restrictions may be imposed by the Chinese authorities, either by way of high import tariffs or non-tariff inspections or standards.
  - o The DM decided not to worry about this risk on the basis (a) that the two-way penalty clause in the contract with the Buyer made this the Buyer's problem to solve if necessary, (b) China has WTO commitments that would be contravened by such actions and (c) the imports would be relatively insignificant so unlikely to attract the attention of the authorities.

- o The sales/purchase contract requires the Buyer to arrange the import of the saddles and to pay any associated import duties, fees and taxes.
- Country (Currency Transfer) Risk. Although China maintains controls over capital transfers there is no reason to believe that payments for imports will be restricted during any relevant period.
  - o China's trade surplus increased to US$ 45.4 billion in October of 2014 from a US$ 31 billion surplus a year earlier, as reported by Business Insider quoting Agence France-Presse (AFP) in November 2014; so its Central Bank does not have a shortage of foreign currency.
  - o The DM is aware that the Buyer must have permission from the Chinese State Administration of Foreign Exchange (SAFE) in order to pay foreign suppliers for imports and is satisfied that the Buyer has the necessary know-how because it is a regular importer of specialised goods.
- Foreign Currency Exchange Risk. DM's Treasurer has confirmed that processes and skills are in place to enable the hedging of exchange risk between the company's currency of accounting, the British Pound (GBP), and the Chinese Renminbi (RMB) also known as the Yuan (CNY).
  - o The DM is aware that the Sales Manager has agreed to invoice these exports in CNY instead of GBP because it is believed that this will help to cement the company's relationship with the Buyer. The latter will be achieved (a) by evidencing respect for the Chinese national currency and (b) by effectively transferring the exchange risk from the Buyer to the Seller. If in future the Buyer is approached by a competitor insisting on invoicing in GBP or USD the Buyer may be disinclined to take on the exchange risk therefore disinclined to handle the competitive brand.
  - o Upon enquiry the DM was informed by Standard Chartered Bank; "Cross-border RMB transactions are

available for goods and service transactions across the whole of mainland China. In June 2012, the RMB trade settlement scheme was expanded to allow all Chinese enterprises with import and export licences to conduct foreign trade in RMB."

- Reputation Risk. There appears to be no reason for the DM to consider this risk in the present context.
  - o The DM's visit to the manufacturer's premises revealed a well-run establishment staffed by obviously motivated employees happily applying their skills. The company's records with Companies House are up to date and taxes have been paid. No derogatory or negative comments about the company were found in the local, national or social media.
  - o No Health and Safety or Environment Impact issues were noted.
- Intellectual Property (IP) Theft Risk perhaps involving 'reverse engineering' the saddles and producing copies more cheaply locally, had to be considered.
  - o While it is clear that 'reverse engineering' of the saddles is certain to be possible the DM thinks it unlikely to occur, for two reasons. The market is highly specialised and therefore probably too small and the profit margin is too unattractive to justify the investment necessary to produce copy saddles.
- Fraud or Theft Risk does not seem to be applicable in this scenario.
- Likewise Deterioration Risk is not a concern since the saddles are not perishable items.
- Buyer Payment Risk also called Post Delivery Risk.
  - o Atradius Credit Information Consulting (Shanghai) Co. Ltd has advised that the Buyer has a good payment track record and is in good standing with its bank, as well as with the local Tax authority.
  - o DM's Credit Team has not approved the 60 day open credit payment terms requested by the Sales Manager. They have explained that the only financial

statements Atradius has been able to obtain (through a local lawyer) are those that the Buyer submitted to its Tax authority, which are not GAAP or IASB-IFRS compliant and not audited. In addition company policy is not to allow payment terms beyond 30 days after despatch of goods. Letter of Credit (LC) payment security opened or confirmed by an acceptable bank and payable 30 days after despatch of the saddles is therefore recommended. The Credit Team does not have any previous experience considering credit applications received from Chinese businesses.

o The DM notes that credit and payment terms were not included in the contract with the Buyer, and on the other hand the contract with Saddlemakers promises payment 30 days after despatch of the goods.

o Therefore DM meets with the Sales Manager to discuss this issue. The latter explains that the Buyer is provided open account terms by several suppliers of other branded goods that it imports, that the cost of opening an LC would reduce the Buyer's net margin and that the Buyer's cash flow cycle is only neutral after 60 days; that is the time elapsing between despatch of the saddles in England and receipt of payment for the sale of the saddles by the Buyer is 60 days. Therefore if the Buyer has to pay in less than 60 days it will have to borrow funds locally to make the payment, thus incurring another profit reducing expense.

o DM calls a fellow member of the Finance Credit and International Business (FCIB) professional association who has experience in dealing with Chinese buyers in a different line of business, for advice.

o The DM subsequently decides to agree the requested 60 day payment terms and open account credit terms.

This decision is based, inter alia, on several considerations including;

- Minimising the Buyer's direct costs and working capital needs creates a more even-handed win-win contract arrangement that is therefore more likely to be respected by the Buyer in the medium to long term.
- Providing credit – working capital financing – related to the transactions helps the Buyer to build a sustainable enterprise that should grow and be enabled to buy more saddles.
- The cost of providing this financing is acceptable given the profit margin built into the sales/purchase contract; moreover it is lower than the cost of administration of the Letters of Credit that are no longer required. Documentary discrepancy risk and potential payment receipt delays related to LC drawings are also avoided.
- The Atradius report confirms that the Buyer receives open account terms from other foreign companies and has a good payment track record.

In conclusion the Decision Maker approves the contract on proviso; that the credit and payment terms offered to the Buyer are added, together with a clause allowing for those terms to be amended or withdrawn at the discretion of the Seller should the Buyer suffer a Material Adverse Change of circumstances or fail to abide by the terms without reasonable cause.

Closing Comments

A Decision Maker experienced in her or his field would in most respects intuitively review the series of risks listed above, rather than working through each one point by point. However all of the aspects would have been given due consideration at some previous time, in similar circumstances; her brain would simply subconsciously provide an answer at each such step.

Therefore an experienced DM can concentrate on considering only those aspects of the proposed transaction that are distinctive.

It is also clear that this decision making process, being by its very nature future orientated, relies heavily on consideration of qualitative information. Numbers, mathematical models and financial ratios are not a focus of the process.

Chapter 8

Scenario Planning

Imagining the Future

A more general way of preparing for the future is by using a technique called Scenario Planning. Utilising this process results in scenarios that are created out of the imagination; based on perceptions of the way in which some important trends may shape the future. Several possible scenarios should be developed.

Scenario Planning is a device that involves composing 'stories about the future', stories that could be possible. However, since the future is entirely unpredictable and often significantly influenced by unforeseen events or inventions, all scenarios are bound to be inaccurate to a greater or lesser extent.

Nevertheless Scenario Planning is an extremely useful tool.

In *How to Build Scenarios* Lawrence Wilkinson explained:

"Scenario planning derives from the observation that, given the impossibility of knowing precisely how the future will play out, a good decision or strategy to adopt is one that plays out well across several possible futures.

To find that robust strategy, scenarios are created in plural, such that each scenario diverges markedly from the others.

Scenario planning allows us to make superior quality plans, by identifying those decisions that 'will make sense across all of the (imagined) futures'.

On the other hand it enables us to identify at an early stage less general changes, to immediately understand the implications of those changes, and to have already mentally rehearsed responses to those changes."

The Scenario Planning Process

Start anticipating the future by understanding the present, recognising major relevant developments and trends. This step is achieved by means of an 'environment scan'.

Consider the impact of aspects of the macro-environment on the chosen subject, including:

- The Natural Environment
- Demographics
- Social Structures
- Government Actions
- Technology developments and
- The National and/or Global Economy

Consider the micro- or industry/market specific environment of the chosen subject, aspects such as:

- Suppliers' bargaining/pricing power
- Potential shortages or surpluses of certain commodities or inputs
- Customers' bargaining power
- Potential substitutes and/or disruptive business models
- Competitive threats from existing rivals or new entrants

Decide which identified elements are 'predetermined' and which are 'critical uncertainties'.

A predetermined element is one that is reasonably predictable; for example we can determine how many 10-year-olds will exist 9 years from now by counting how many babies were born last year.

On the other hand a critical uncertainty is an element that cannot be accurately predicted but is likely to have a major impact should it arise. The technical advances being made in respect of the generation and storage of solar power – either by use of advanced battery technologies and/or producing biogas from algae or biomass – for instance will probably displace the role of coal in the production of electricity but it is difficult to be certain when this will occur.

When the research is complete, there are two possible optional or complimentary scenario drafting approaches, namely; the Top Down approach or the Bottom Up approach:

Writing a 'Top Down Scenario':

1. Consider the focus or subject of the scenario; for example the industry or market in which you are currently active, like the 'energy sector' or 'tourism' or 'education' or 'employment'.

2. In your mind, picture yourself sitting at home on a day, say, 10 or 20 years in the future.

3. Then compose a letter to a friend describing the important business changes that have taken place in the last, say, 10 or 20 years, and how the industry or market and daily life has changed.

4. Analyse the inherent significant uncertainties described in the letter. Consider the implications of each in respect of current decision making and planning.

Writing a 'Bottom Up Scenario':

1. Working with an interest group, formulate the Scenario Question to be answered; the subject of the scenario.

2. Identify the relevant significant Driving Forces at play.

3. Polarise the driving forces to formulate discrete scenarios.

4. Form sub-groups, each to elaborate one scenario.

5. Discuss the elaborated scenarios as a group.

6. Consider the implications of each scenario in respect of current decision making and planning.

An instructive example of the art of Scenario Planning is provided in the book *Russia 2010 and what it means for the World* by Daniel Yergin and Thane Gustafson. In the opening chapter the authors provide a full explanation of the process they employed and then go on to elaborate three distinct scenarios.

In order to illustrate the Scenario Building Process an example is presented here:

An Example Top Down Scenario

How will our 9.2 billion neighbours be gainfully employed in 2035?

TWENTY YEARS OF CHANGE:

Despite all the writings, TED Talks, and news items repeating that change had already changed, even before the Second Millennium commenced, no one seeking to imagine the future in early 2015 properly understood the enormity of the change we have experienced over the past 20 years.

As far back as 2000 in *Leading the Revolution* Gary Hamel began his campaign to persuade business managers and employees that:

"We now stand on the threshold of a new age – the age of revolution. In our minds we know the new age has already arrived; in our bellies, we're not sure we like it. For we know it is going to be an age of upheaval, of tumult, of fortunes made and unmade at head-snapping speed. The Age of Progress is over, for change has changed. No longer is it (additional), no longer does it move in a straight line. In the twenty-first century, change is discontinuous, abrupt, (and) seditious."

However little in terms of corporate structures, business models and management practices had changed when Ken Blanchard, in 2009 in *Leading at a Higher Level* wrote:

"Today we live in 'permanent white-water'. It's both exhilarating and scary! You often have to go sideways or upside down to go forward. The flow is controlled by the environment. There are unseen obstacles. Occasionally it's wise to use an eddy to regroup and reflect, but eddies are often missed because the white-water seems to create its own momentum."

In 2012, Gary Hamel continued his campaign by publishing *What Matters Now: How to Win in a World of Relentless Change, Ferocious Competition and Unstoppable Innovation*, but sadly the majority of business leaders where so fixated on watching their enormous bank balances grow that they ignored his sage advice. Many employees paid the price of their leaders' navel-gazing greed, losing their jobs as disruptive technologies, new business models, demographic and social changes swamped their businesses.

In her seminal work *How the West Was Lost: Fifty Years of Economic Folly* (published in 2011) Dambisa Moyo wrote:

"There are two aspects of labour that affect a country's ability to excel as an economic market: one is quantity and other quality – and on both counts the West is holding a losing hand. In the first instance, it is a matter of simple demographics. (In the) second, a characteristic of emerging economies is the fact that a large proportion of their populations is young; (representing) a well-stocked pool of labour, ready and willing to learn new skills and staff new industries."

However the TED Talk by Andrew McAfee, titled *What will future jobs look like?*, rather 'put the spanner in the works' for the emerging economies, see: http://on.ted.com/j0JVk. In this talk McAfee explained;

86

"Yes, probably, droids will take our jobs — or at least the kinds of jobs we know now."

In this far-seeing talk, he thought through what future jobs might look like, and how to educate coming generations to hold them. Fortunately progressive education establishments such as the United World College of South East Asia (Singapore) created the approaches necessary to develop 21st Century global citizens equipped to make valuable contributions to society.

As robotics and the use of 3D Printing for manufacture of a wide range of consumer goods and spare parts advanced, so most menial jobs disappeared; hence workers in the emerging countries were not spared unemployment.

As predicted by Mark Stevenson, author of *An Optimist's Tour of the Future*, when interviewed in 2011; "the interplay of infotech, nanotech and biotech…blurring together sometimes, (created) hyper-exponential growth" in advances in technologies and the realisation of solutions to important challenges, such as how to develop sufficient renewable sources of energy to eliminate the use of the worst fossil-fuel polluter coal.

Gerd Leonhard, as reported by Steve Porter of INNOVATIONEWS almost 25 years ago, has been proven to have been correct when he said;

"Just having a job in the future will be a challenge…as machines take over more and more menial work. The key to having a job in the future is to be able to do something machines can't do. If you're a therapist, a cook, a negotiator, an artistic director – you may have a job."

Paraphrasing what Rowan Gibson, et alia, wrote in *Rethinking the Future*;

"The nature of work (didn't) change. The nature of the (status didn't) change. It's rather the individual's ability and the degree of sophistication that he or she is able to bring to the job that (has changed), and the complexity of the situations that he or she is able to handle."

As Arnold Geelhoed described in his article *A World Shaped by 3D Printing* in 2013;

"Creators, Innovators, Engineers, Designers, Chemists and Nano-Technologists will be 'the new heroes' (of the future workforce) providing the designs and the materials required to make 3D Printing (local manufacturing of single items) a cost effective and practical reality for many millions of people."

The branch of Nano-Technology that is referred to here is that which involves the creation of new materials by manipulating the atomic structure of existing substances, such as carbon.

As we consider the employment scene in 2035 we have to acknowledge that Seth Godin gave fair warning as long ago as 2010 – in *Linchpin: How to Drive Your Career and Create a Remarkable Future* – when he observed;

"Organisations will always strive to replace replaceable elements with cheaper substitutes. I grew up in a world where people did what they were told, followed instructions, found a job, made a living and that was that. Now we live in a world where all the joy and profit have been squeezed out of following the rules. Outsourcing and automation and the new marketing punish anyone who is merely good, merely obedient, and merely reliable. It doesn't matter if you're a wedding photographer or an insurance broker; there's no longer a clear path to satisfaction in working for the man. The factory – that system where organised labour meets patient capital, productivity-improving devices, and leverage – has fallen apart.

Here's the problem, which you've already guessed. If you make a business possible to replicate, you're not going to be the one to replicate it. Others will. If you build a business filled with rules and procedures that are designed to allow you to hire cheap people, you will have to produce a product without humanity or personalisation or connection. (This) means that you'll have to lower your prices to compete. (This) leads to a race to the bottom. Indispensable businesses race to the top instead."

Lynda Gratton in her book *The Shift: The Future of Work is Already Here* published in 2011 noted;

"In a world of more and more complex technology, it is the highly skilled employees, or what I will call those with mastery, who will always find work." Writing about the year 2025 she continued later; "With the emergence of mega-cities, instead of connected parts the suburbs are increasingly becoming slums. Far from claiming their own purpose and identity, these concentrated areas of 'surplus humanity' exhibit intense poverty and little direction. This disconnection has been exacerbated by vast urbanisation that has seen millions of people leave the land, hoping for a better life in the cities. As the slums around Mumbai or Johannesburg will attest, these hopes are rarely realised."

THE RESULT IS WHAT WE OBSERVE IN 2035:

The spectre of vast numbers of 'surplus humanity' eking out a living in slums and creating a disaffected underclass of billions of people caused most nation states to radically revise their economic and governance models. Referencing the apocryphal divergent stories of Ted – the college educated professional or technical worker – and Bill - the clerical worker – as told by Andrew McAfee in the TED Talk mentioned above, many nations beyond Europe introduced the 'guaranteed minimum income' concept.

Most societies have turned away from the 'winner takes all' approach to life to follow the Singapore approach that emphasises inclusivity and promoting harmony within the community. China's success in urbanising hundreds of millions of people while avoiding vast slums developing has also provided many countries with ideas that have proved successful.

Mass employment has been created by the spontaneous formation of many cooperative ventures aided (a) by the demand for customised goods and (b) person-to-person connectivity courtesy of the World Wide Web; to which almost seven billion people now have access.

In *The Shift*, Lynda Gratton described a day in the life of Xui Li, Bao Yu and Chenh-Gong in 2025. These fictional micro-entrepreneurs marshalled an 'army' of embroiderers (some 10,000 business partners) each of whom worked at home to fulfil small customised orders.

Freelance working is another development that has led to millions of people finding rewarding and personally fulfilling employment; albeit through execution of, or participation in a series of short or medium term assignments or projects.

Innovators like Jack Hughes, the founder of TopCoder, and James DeJulio, co-founder and president of Tongal are credited with initiating this development as long ago as 2014.

TopCoder was the world's largest community of software developers and digital creators, and Tongal the world's first virtual studio on-demand for creation of viral advertising videos; as described via this link: mixmashup.org/video/jack-hughes-james-dejulio-mashup-talk.

THE SOCIAL ORDER HAS ALSO CHANGED:

The tremendous changes we have experienced have not only impacted national and international organisations and government structures. They have led to a root and branch revision of the economic model of growth that was based for a hundred years on the combination of liberal democracy and private capitalism; the model that formerly catapulted Western countries to new levels of economic development.

Dambisa Moyo (renowned global economist and author) in her TEDGlobal talk in June 2013 made a number of prescient points that proved to be accurate as the last 21 years passed. Her talk can be viewed at http://go.ted.com/snn.

Ms Moyo's most telling points included:

"On balance, (people in non-Western nations) worry more about where their living standard improvements are going to come from, and how it is their governments can deliver for them, than whether or not the government was elected by democracy.

The fact of the matter is that this has become a very poignant question because there is for the first time in a long time a real challenge to the Western ideological systems of politics and economics, and this is a system that is embodied by China. Rather than have private capitalism, (China has) state capitalism. Instead of liberal democracy, they have de-prioritised the democratic system. Furthermore they have decided to prioritise economic rights over political rights. I put it to you today that it is this system, embodied by China, which is gathering momentum.

(The current generation is) looking at China and saying; 'China can produce infrastructure, China can produce economic growth, and we like that.'

Around the world, people are pointing at what China is doing and saying, 'I like that. I want that. I want to be able to do

what China's doing. That is the system that seems to work.'
I'm here to tell you that there are lots of shifts occurring
around what China is doing in the democratic (sphere). In
particular, there is growing doubt among people in the
emerging markets, (where) people now believe that
democracy is no longer to be viewed as a prerequisite for
economic growth.

The question before seven billion people on the planet is;
how can we create prosperity? People who care will, in a
very rational way pivot towards the model of politics and
economics that will ensure that they can have better living
standards in the shortest period of time."

Ketan J Patel, writing in *The Master Strategist* in 2005,
earnestly expressed the hope that the global community could
agree that its collective purpose would be "the pursuit of peace,
prosperity and freedom" for the benefit of all the World's
citizens. In this respect the new economic order in 2035 has
prioritised development on the understanding that there can be
no sustainable freedom without prosperity; it is nonetheless
understood that peace is a precondition of prosperity.

The first third of the 21st Century has certainly been "an age of
upheaval, of tumult, of fortunes made and unmade at head-
snapping speed" but humanity has met the many challenges
with technical ingenuity, economic model adjustments and
social reforms that augur well for the future.

RISKS THAT INJURE REAL BUSINESSES

Other than macro- and micro- Black Swan events there are three classes of risk that may attack and injure real businesses, by causing losses. Generally executives are prepared to effectively deal with these risks using tried and tested techniques. This section covers the most common forms of these risks.

Chapter 9

Unknown Knowns – Common Business Risks

Introduction

Common Business Risks are unwelcome outcomes that have happened in the past, so data is available from which insurers, banks (financial institutions) and businesses can calculate (a) the probability of a similar incident occurring in future [probability of loss] and (b) the likely related direct financial loss [expected loss]. To that extent they are 'known' risks.

On the other hand there is no way of identifying which particular item of asset or sub-group of assets, within a portfolio of at-risk-assets, will be lost or when the loss will occur. In that respect they are 'unknown' risks.

Statistical Risk Management

'Probability of Loss' is an important component of the statistical risk management approach but it is only useful in the context of a reasonable size portfolio of individual risks or assets. The probability is usually expressed as a percentage, which purports to indicate the loss likely to arise within a certain time period.

In fact effective statistical risk management depends on a portfolio view of baskets of similar assets because the concepts used are probabilistic, thus their meaning is expressed in the aggregate.

Therefore, in respect of a single asset, a 1% risk of complete loss within a year is not very meaningful, except to indicate that this asset is less at risk than one that has a 15% probability of loss, for example.

If the asset in question is lost (written off) then 100% of its value will be lost; not 1%.

However if it is part of a group, for instance, of 100 similar assets with an overall risk of loss of 1%, the amount expected to be written off during the year will be the value of one of the constituent individual assets; that is 1% of the total portfolio value. Nevertheless which particular asset will be lost is unknown at the start of the period.

In respect of most routine business risks, entities may either purchase insurance cover or 'self-insure'. Usually businesses choose a mixed approach.

Whether a business 'self-insures' or purchases insurance from an underwriting company or syndicate, such as Lloyds of London, insurance only works in relation to portfolios of risks. This is based on the understanding that the income derived from each constituent asset, be that net profit in the case of self-insurance or premiums in the case of purchased insurance, will be sufficient to cover the expected loss that will be incurred; **if** the probability of loss calculation is accurate.

Therefore a domestic household removal company that operates one van can avoid retaining the risk that it would lose 100% of the value of the van, should it be written-off, by purchasing insurance. This action would in effect add its single van to a portfolio of *at risk transport vehicles* that the insurance company already covers. The insurer, in return for offering to reimburse the business the full current value of its van if it is lost, would require payment of a premium. The amount of the premium would be based on a percentage of the value of the van related to the associated 'probability of loss'; say 1% in this example. In this way the insurer would receive enough in aggregate premium income, from the owners of the portfolio constituent vehicles, to cover its 'expected loss' of one vehicle.

On the other hand a company that operates a fleet of 100 vans, with an overall 'probability of loss' of 1% would avoid paying 100 times 1% of the cost of a van in insurance premiums by opting to self-insure. However it would bear the statistical risk that one of its vans may be written-off during the year. In order to reduce the chance of loss the company would operate prudent policies regarding the maintenance of the fleet, operating standards and driver qualifications required. In that way the company would strive to avoid paying annual premiums equivalent to the cost of one van.

Self-insurance

Businesses that self-insure do so employing a combination of expertise, discipline and hedging, plus systems and procedures in order to assess, avoid and/or constraint inherent risks; while generating reserves to cover any losses incurred.

Reserves are accumulated;

(a) by avoiding paying insurance premiums and by incurring losses at a rate less than the statistical average – since businesses are often in a better position than their insurers to assess and to minimise their own risks – and/or

(b) as additional profits are earned by charging higher risk customers a risk premium; while avoiding losses on the basis of superior customer knowledge and relationships.

Purchased Insurance

In a similar manner, when a business purchases insurance it nevertheless employs expertise, discipline, systems and procedures but in this case (a) to limit premiums paid, (b) to ensure that any claims will be accepted by the underwriter and paid, and (c) to avoid having to maintain reserves or borrow cash to cover losses.

Most businesses use a combination of purchased and self-insurance depending on the nature of each class of risk carried and the in-house or specialist-advisor expertise available to assess and manage each risk.

Nevertheless, as pointed out in the opening chapters, it must be borne in mind that as in life, in business the inherent risks cannot be eliminated. However they can be transformed into more manageable and/or less risky varieties. Transformation of a risk may be worthwhile if the cost involved is outweighed by the perceived risk reduction effect.

The Common Business Risk Circle

The above diagram illustrates that common business risks sit on a base of certain underlying risks; Country Risk (foreign currency transfer and exchange risk), Regulation and Compliance Risks, Concentration and Correlation Risks, and Fraud and Theft Risks, for example.

Central and overarching are Reputation Risk and Change Risks.

The grey portion of the diagram records the risks most commonly carried by a physical enterprise in the normal course of business.

97

Market or Price Risk

When supplies of raw materials, other resources and/or inventory are contracted there is a risk that ordered items may not be received. This could be due to loss or destruction in transit or failure of the supplier. The result may be a loss incurred obtaining replacement material at a higher than budgeted price and/or missed sales due to production or availability disruption.

Similarly when selling specialised products still to be produced or contracting to deliver services at fixed prices in future, changes in related costs could result in losses being incurred. Likewise a loss would result if a buyer failed to take delivery of a specialised product.

Market risk can be managed using 'hedging techniques' discussed in previous chapters, however hedging gives rise to Performance Risk.

Credit Risk

Performance Risk is the division of Credit Risk that arises out of the act of trusting another party, be that a supplier or buyer, to meet its contract obligation to supply or take delivery of goods or services at an agreed future time, at a pre-agreed price.

This risk can be managed utilising 'margining' arrangements, which incur Operational Risk.

Post Delivery Payment Risk is the other division of Credit Risk. Payment risk arises when payment terms, other than 'payment in advance' or 'cash on delivery', are granted to a buyer. That is when a business trusts its customer to pay for goods at some agreed date after they are delivered. The customer is in effect given an 'option to default' unless the supplier requires it to provide collateral or a guarantee to cover the amount due, should it fail to pay. The taking of collateral or a guarantee gives rise to Operational Risk.

Operational Risk

Margining incorporates both Liquidity Risk, as discussed in Chapter 3, and the risk that administrative or calculation errors will cause losses. Additionally Legal Risks may be inherent if the associated bipartite agreement is not correctly drafted.

Taking of guarantees (often in the form of Documentary or Standby Letters of Credit) incurs contingent Payment Risk against the guarantee providers. Documentary Risk may also arise in that claim documents may be rejected and fail to trigger payment due to errors.

Other operational risks, such as those associated with transport and storage of goods, cyber security and export-import regulations could be sparked due to administrative errors as well as natural causes.

Such risks will often be insured, resulting in Insurer or Underwriter Risk.

Collateral Risk

In the case of a contingent payment obligation, as mentioned, a combination of third-party Bank/Insurer, Legal and/or Documentary Risk results.

However if physical collateral is taken, perhaps in the form of a pledge of a quantity of a commodity (a base or precious metal for example) the value of the collateral will be determined by the internationally quoted reference price, and will change from time to time. As a result the risk transformation process reverts back to Price or Market Risk.

Liens

A form of quasi-physical collateral that may come into being in the normal course of business is a lien; that is the right to keep possession of another's property until a related debt owed by the owner is paid.

Examples of liens that arise in the course of business are a *mechanic's lien* and a *maritime lien*. In many jurisdictions, for example, a person who repairs a vehicle has the right to retain possession of the vehicle until the repair bill is paid.

In certain jurisdictions the supplier of fuel to a ship may evoke a maritime lien in order to achieve the arrest (constructive possession) of the ship, to ensure it is held in port until the debt for the fuel is paid.

Naturally the market value of the property held under a lien versus the value of the debt due will determine the effectiveness of the lien in ensuring payment; hence asset value or market risk is innate.

Common Business Risk Lists

Lists of Common Business Risks that are insurable and/or may be managed in-house (self-insured) include:

Operational Risk
Regulation Risk
Legal Risk
Documentary Risk
Administrative Error Risk
Fire and Water Damage
Traffic or Train Accident
Sinking of a Ship
Aircraft Accident

Credit Risk
Supplier Performance Risk
Customer Performance Risk
Customer Post Delivery Payment Risk
Country Risk, including boycott or sanctions
Bank Failure Risk – also a Financial Risk

Financial Risk
  Bank Failure Risk
  Foreign Exchange Rate Risk
  Country Lack of Foreign Currency Risk – also a Credit Risk
  Fraud and Theft Risk – including Intellectual Property (IP) theft
  Regulation Compliance Risk
  Reputation Risk – including Customer and Employee Data theft
  Death or Disability of Key Employees

Submissions

Recommended and widely used methods for in-house management of Credit and Financial Risks in physical businesses are well covered in business publications. For example *Global Credit Management – An Executive Summary*, published by John Wiley and Sons, covers Customer Risk, Country Risk and Bank Risk assessment and management succinctly.

Currently articles appear regularly in business journals and blogs covering Reputation Risk, Regulation Compliance Risk and Cyber Security Risk; which indicates that a body of knowledge pertinent to real businesses is being developed in each of these disciplines.

On the other hand Operational Risk (OR) management techniques are not well reported, possibly because OR is not a cohesive subject. It is also difficult to *silo* this discipline since its impact extends across the whole business. As mentioned in Chapter 4, operational risk encompasses a variety of risk types, some of which are avoidable by means of adopting standards and procedures. Some elements of risk can be limited by ensuring involved employees have adequate experience and training, others by diversifying sources or means of transport. Several aspects of operational risk can be mitigated by purchasing insurance; fire and water damage for example.

Others are resolved by having good relationships with the third parties involved in the supply chain; based on win-win contracts that encourage all participants to work together to solve the problems that arise.

Stress Testing

Common Business Risks result in outcomes that can be imagined, since examples have occurred in the past. Stress Testing may be used to assist any contingency planning process. The probability that the studied risk or risks may occur is simply exaggerated in order to develop various scenarios.

For example, as mentioned in Chapter 3, stress testing cash flow forecasts is an important and very useful activity that should be carried out frequently. This should include exaggerating foreign exchange (forex) rate movements to check the cash impact, if the business has foreign currency direct and/or forex related derivative exposures.

Any complex derivative positions could result in devastating losses if not carefully analysed and frequently reviewed. Positions such as the 'Knock-in Knock-out' (KiKo) arrangement that destroyed numerous Korean exporters should be modelled and stress tested. KiKo positions soured when the expectation that the Korean Won would continue a two year trend of strengthening against the US Dollar abruptly reversed in 2008.

Instead of more expensive simple swaps, Korean businesses were sold KiKos by their banks – since they were cheaper. KiKos were call- and put-option combinations that protected businesses if the USD continued to weaken against the KRW (Won); by preserving the KRW value of exports priced in USD. However when the USD strengthened against the KRW, the potential loss was unlimited and drove the many entities that 'overlooked' this possibility to bankruptcy.

**Poetic
Summary**

Risk is the Context of Life
The Chameleon in the Room

Decision Making
Is Risk Taking
Outcomes are
Unpredictable

But to avoid a Risk
Is to Risk
Opportunity Missed

The Future does not Exist
Only the Present Exists
One moment at a time

So to assess a Risk
Then embrace the Risk
Is to make a Bold Decision
Decisions Sway the Future

THE FUTURE
Past Decisions Constrained
Brave Decisions Shaped
Major Impact Events Jolted
Embraces a New Present
One Moment at a Time

Bibliography

How Different Cultures Understand Time by Richard Lewis of Richard Lewis Communications, a Business Insider Article published June 1, 2014

Life's a Pitch by S Bayley & R Mavity, publisher Corgi September 2008 ISBN: 978-0552156837

Mastery by Robert Greene, publisher Profile Books November 2012 ISBN: 978-1781250914

Managing Extreme Financial Risk - Strategies and Tactics for Going Concerns by Karamjeet Paul, publisher Elsevier Inc September 2013
ISBN: 978-0124172210

Managing Risk to Avoid Supply-Chain Breakdown by Sunil Chopra and ManMohan S. Sodhi, article published by MIT Sloan Management Review October 15, 2004 See: http://sloanreview.mit.edu

How to Build Scenarios by Lawrence Wilkinson 1994-98, a Wired Digital Inc article

Russia 2010 and what it means for the World by Daniel Yergin & Thane Gustafson © 1993, 1995, publisher Cambridge Energy Research Associates
ISBN: 978-0679429951

The Black Swan: The Impact of the Highly Improbable by Nassim Nicholas Taleb, publisher Penguin February 2008 ISBN: 978-0141034591

The Liquidity Management Guide: from Policy to Pitfalls by Gudni Adalsteinsson, publisher Wiley Finance Series June 2014 ISBN: 978-1118858004

Drive: The Surprising Truth about What Motivates Us by Daniel H Pink, publisher Canongate Books Ltd; Main edition January 2011 ISBN: 978-1847677693

Leading the Revolution by Gary Hamel, publisher Harvard Business Review Press, Revised 2002 ISBN: 978-1591391463

Leading at a Higher Level, Revised and Expanded Edition: Blanchard on Leadership and Creating High Performing Organizations by Ken Blanchard, publisher Pearson FT Press 2009 ISBN: 978-0137011704

What Matters Now: How to Win in a World of Relentless Change, Ferocious Competition and Unstoppable Innovation by Gary Hamel, publisher Jossey-Bass 2012 ISBN: 978-1118120828

How the West Was Lost: Fifty Years of Economic Folly and the Stark Choices Ahead by Dambisa Moyo, publisher Farrar, Straus and Giroux 2011 ISBN: 978-0374533212

What will future jobs look like? A TED Talk by Andrew McAfee, to view use this link: http://on.ted.com/j0JVk

An Optimist's Tour of the Future: One Curious Man Sets Out to Answer "What's Next?" by Mark Stevenson, publisher Profile Books Ltd 2011 ISBN: 978-1846683572

Built to Reinvent: The Ten Commandments of Today's Sustainable Company by Nadya Zhexembayeva, Issue 128.02 provided by ChangeThis.com April 2015

Rethinking the Future: Rethinking Business, Principles, Competition, Control & Complexity, Leadership, Markets and the World by Rowan Gibson (Author), Rowana Gibson (Editor), Alvin Toffler (Foreword), Heidi Toffler (Foreword), Charles Handy (Contributor), Stephen Covey (Contributor),

Michael Porter (Contributor), C K Prahalad (Contributor), Kindle version publisher Nicholas Brealey Publishing 2011 ASIN: B005CI9GKK

A World Shaped by 3D Printing this article by Arnold Geelhoed in 2013, is available with permission of the National Association of Credit Management (NACM), via:
http://www.barrettwells.co.uk/3DPrintingBCJulAug13AGeelhoed.pdf

Linchpin: Are You Indispensable? How to drive your career and create a remarkable future by Seth Godin, publisher Piatkus 2010 ASIN: B00DJG4224

The Shift: The Future of Work is Already Here by Lynda Gratton, publisher HarperCollins Business 2011 ISBN: 978-0007427956

Is China the new (hero) for emerging economies? A TEDGlobal Talk by Dambisa Moyo, June 2013, to view use this link: http://go.ted.com/snn

The Master Strategist: Power, Purpose and Principle by Ketan J Patel, publisher Hutchinson 2005 ISBN: 978-1844138173

The Sharing Company - Behind the hype of peer-to-peer economics is a quiet B2B revolution by Robert Vaughan, published: October 28, 2014 by PWC Strategy & LLC See: www.strategy-business.com

Global Credit Management – an Executive Summary by Ron Wells, publisher John Wiley & Sons January 2004 ISBN: 978-0470851111 See: http://www.barrettwells.com/gcm.html

Other Risk Management Resources at:
http://www.barrettwells.co.uk and http://www.barrettwells.com

OTHER PUBLISHED BOOKS BY THIS AUTHOR:

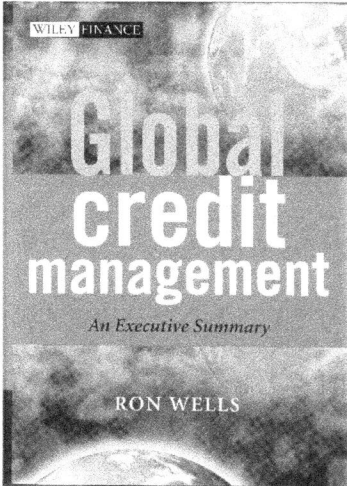

ISBN: 978-0-470-85111-1

ISBN: 978-988-99586-1-9

Paperback ISBN: 978-0-9576279-2-5
eBook ISBN: 978-0-9576279-0-1
All books are available through
http://www.t3plimited.com/estore.html

Appreciation

In relation to the new risk management ideas that I have innovated and described in this book, I am particularly grateful for the inspiration I gained from Karamjeet Paul.

Initially I was reminded of the pressing need to understand, measure and manage Extreme Risk Events reading Mr Paul's book *Managing Extreme Financial Risk - Strategies and Tactics for Going Concerns*. The focus of his book and subsequent articles is on Financial Institutions; whereas I was motivated to consider the subject in relation to non-financial institutions. Subsequent 'conversations' with Mr Paul and his mention of the Philips Albuquerque case convinced me to apply my mind to this subject.

It was from this rootstock, shaped by my own challenging and fun experiences gained making risk decisions and creating solutions in real businesses - together with ideas gleaned from a number of other authors and former colleagues - that *The Chameleon in the Room* grew into the nine branch tree in your hands.

Ron Wells

www.ingramcontent.com/pod-product-compliance
Lightning Source LLC
Chambersburg PA
CBHW071505200326
41519CB00019B/5880